P9-DEQ-891

BY THE SAME AUTHOR

The Golden Age of Promiscuity

City Poet: The Life and Times of Frank O'Hara

Scary Kisses

Jailbait and Other Stories

The Daily News

FINDING THE BOYFRIEND WITHIN

A Practical Guide for Tapping into
Your Own Source of Love,
Happiness, and Respect

BRAD GOOCH

Simon & Schuster Paperbacks

New York   London   Toronto Sydney

Simon & Schuster Paperbacks
Rockefeller Center
1230 Avenue of the Americas
New York, NY 10020

Copyright © 1999 by Brad Gooch

All rights reserved, including the right of reproduction
in whole or in part in any form.

SIMON & SCHUSTER PAPERBACKS and colophon are
registered trademarks of Simon & Schuster, Inc.

For information about special discounts for bulk purchases,
please contact Simon & Schuster Special Sales:
1-800-456-6798 or business@simonandschuster.com

Designed by Ruth Lee

Manufactured in the United States of America

9   10   8

The Library of Congress has cataloged the hardcover
edition as follows:
Gooch, Brad.
Finding the boyfriend within / Brad Gooch.
p.   cm.
1. Gay men—Psychology. 2. Single men—Psychology.
3. Male friendship. I. Title.
HQ76.25.G66   1999
305.38'9664—dc21   98-50441
ISBN-13: 978-0-684-85040-5
ISBN-10:   0-684-85040-0
ISBN-13: 978-0-7432-2530-4 (Pbk)
ISBN-10:   0-7432-2530-9 (Pbk)

Special thanks to Barbara Heizer, for thoughtfully reading this book in manuscript; to Geoff Freitag, Bill Katz, Wayne Nathan, and Mary Michael Simpson for their encouragement and anecdotes; to my editor, Chuck Adams, and my agent, Joy Harris.

FINDING THE
BOYFRIEND WITHIN

INTRODUCTION

Here's the situation: I'm in my mid-forties. Everyone says I look ten years younger, more or less. I'm gay, but extremely flexible and historically not too worried, ashamed, or complicated about my predilections. (I don't remember the phrase "coming out" even going through my head when I decided to get on with my romantic life in my late teens.)

I had a lover, Howard. When I was twenty-five, and he was twenty-three, we met at an innocuous, somewhat preppy gay bar in the Village misleadingly named The Ninth Circle—there were at least a half dozen bars in Manhattan in 1978 much more deserving to be named after the final circle of Hell. We didn't go home with each other that night. (Nearly a first, at the time, for me.) Howard and I were involved as lovers for eleven years, until his death from AIDS in 1989. I miss him so much more than I ever thought I would. Somehow we stumbled into a kind of natural, brotherly camaraderie and a love that suited both of us. Actually, I thought my life would always be like that. If not with Howard, then with someone else.

I can now say that I've definitely discovered that my expectation of an easy replacement was way off. Since Howard's death I've been involved with three different boyfriends. Each was twenty-eight when I met him. Each rumbled through a thirtieth birthday during our time together. Each was different, but each was a roller-coaster ride of a sort. All were work. None was a match made in heaven. In every case, we parted ways after two or three years—twice, rambunctiously;

once, with no hard feelings as things just gradually ended with a sigh of indifference. All three were handsome, sexy catches. But as the guidebooks say, sex isn't love. And neither, I might add, is curiosity. Or acquisitiveness. Or style.

A break in this pattern came during a New Year's Eve celebration at an ashram in upstate New York, where I was researching a book I was writing at the time. I was there to work, not to commune. With my red notebook in hand and my sensitive antennae stretched way up, I felt safe and impervious. I had a job to do. "Not like the rest of these gullible, New Age softies, concentrating on their mantras," I thought. But all the sitting and meditating finally affected even me. It was as if my insides opened up and I found myself in a cave with blue-purple lighting—a secure place where I enjoyed spending time and even became pleasantly lost. The experience wasn't totally alien. I'd been there before at different times in my life. I can remember once when I was six years old zoning out in a similar den of Ali Baba's thieves. For many years, though, I hadn't visited this alluring cave of solitude.

My forty-fifth birthday arrived a few weeks after my visit to the ashram. Soon afterward I stopped drinking, stopped smoking (the little that I had), was meditating twice a day, seeing my therapist at eight o'clock one morning and working out with my trainer at nine the next. My research on this spiritual book was leading me down a winding road that included releasing toxins at the Chopra Center for Well Being in La Jolla; reading books such as *Conversations with God,* by Neale Donald Walsch; attending a different church every Sunday. (My favorite was Saint Francis Xavier Roman Catholic church, because it had the cutest guys.)

I felt as if I had been given a shiny new deck of cards and had been told to start dealing. Secretly, I of course assumed that hidden away in this deck would be the Prince of Hearts: the boyfriend card. It was almost as if in some replay of the corny old making-a-deal-with-God scenario, I expected that if I cleaned up my act, I was going to be rewarded with a boyfriend who was successful, handsome, full of character, and, this time, with an aura of spirituality. I secretly believed that this was an unsigned, unspoken, entirely understood (by whom?) package deal. Well, the Prince of Hearts card was never played. Not even the Two of Hearts turned up. Just the opposite occurred. Every bit of sex, romance, titillation, flirting, and dating in my life went entirely flat. . . . What could be more unfair?

Something else *was* more unfair. The old solu-

tions for finding love in all the wrong places—the con-
solation prizes, as it were—didn't satisfy anymore.
They didn't even work when I did revert to old habits,
when I was jones-ing for love, as it were. I used to be
able to place imaginative ads on phone-sex lines that
would immediately be answered by hot-to-trot respondents. Suddenly the special service number I kept
exclusively for such anonymous admirers was not
worth its $9 monthly fee. I used to be able to walk into
a local leather bar and feel like Sharon Stone in her
Gap T-shirt cruising into the Academy Awards. Suddenly it was as if I wasn't even there. No more eye contact. (Not drinking didn't help in diving into those
fast-moving currents.) My heart just wasn't into visiting the dirty-movie theater where I had spent so many
earth-opening—or so they seemed to me—evenings
when I was the porn critic for a now-defunct New York
City gay newspaper.

I didn't find a foxy stranger, or a boyfriend either.
But I did find at that time the inspiration for this
book. One evening I was downstairs—I live on the top
floor of a four-story house in SoHo—at a party given
by good friends and neighbors. They're a straight couple who were about to be married in June. A guest of
theirs arrived with his new boyfriend. Both are film
agents who live in L.A.

The new boyfriend said to me: "I've heard so much about you. I've been at so many dinners where people talked about you. How great-looking you are. What a good writer you are. What a nice guy you are. I see these little inch-by-inch photos of you in gossip columns and magazines. I'm glad to finally meet you."

"Why thank you," I answered graciously.

"But tell me, do you have a boyfriend?" he asked, leadingly.

"No."

"Well, I guess then it's all worth nothing," he responded.

"Ummmm. . . ." Long pause. "Let's not throw out the baby with the bath water. . . . What about the boyfriend within?"

"Yeah, people say things like that. But I never believe them."

His comment felt like a smack. I'm sure he was simply being unintentionally spastic. But I was challenged to try to formulate a response, to try to explain what I really meant. My first attempts, in my head of course, produced only clichés. As I replayed the scene for the third, fourth time over the next five, six weeks, though, a tingle of good feeling began percolating.

Slowly I understood more fully what I'd meant when I blurted out my quick comeback about "the boyfriend within." I was simply reaching—in a contemporary, gay way—back to an ancient idea that informs all of the traditions of wisdom with which I'm familiar, both Eastern and Western. It was the simple truth that love, happiness, and respect come from within. What we often mean when we say, "I'm looking for a boyfriend," is that we're looking for that warm feeling of happiness, or contentment, or peace and inner satisfaction, for that turning of the heart into a pond of golden nectar. Of course this sense of love, happiness, and integrity traditionally arises out of a relationship with someone else. Other people provide endless opportunities for us to extend ourselves, to reach out, to "get over ourselves." But the basic, often-mouthed-yet-still-true paradox is that we're only good at loving and being happy with others to the extent that we love and are happy being with ourselves. The Boyfriend Within is made up of our own inner qualities, considered and respected. Yet it's surprising how often such self-appreciation—as distinct from self-centeredness—is lacking.

The stranger across the crowded room is often just a mirror in which we're really seeing some of our own best qualities, the qualities of our Boyfriend Within. We project these qualities outward. We imagine that we see in the mirror of the other person someone who is going to be loving, caring, understanding, protective, stimulating, supportive, exciting; someone who will take care of us when we're down, put his arm around our shoulders during stressful periods or emergencies, and, best of all, keep us titillated and surprised and feeling sexy in the most general way all the time. What we often don't realize is that this imaginary lover is inside ourselves. And it's one of the standard mysteries of life that when we locate that tall, dark, wise, and handsome lover within ourselves, he's more likely to materialize out of that mirror and become an actual three-dimensional good guy in our lives—though always a bit less controlled and perfect than the man in the mirror. Halls of mirrors are fun for a while, but ultimately they're frustrating. Better to experience the relaxation and growing satisfaction that comes from the real thing, the Boyfriend Within. Then, even if life doesn't provide a matching fund in the form of a new beau, or a longtime companion perceived in a new light, you won't really mind so much. I promise.

As I was going to bed one night during my season of questioning, I realized this absence of contentment in myself quite strongly. I noticed that two pairs of beat-up sneakers and lots of dirty white socks were strewn next to my futon bed. The bed itself was covered with numerous sections of the Sunday *Times*. Sheets and blankets were rolling in contradictory directions. There was a crusty cereal bowl nestled between two misshapen pillows. The alarm didn't need to be reset since I'd overused its "snooze" option sixteen hours earlier. The shade had snapped to the top of the window, where it was likely to remain, only to be cursed the next morning when the sun began to glare.

I was prepared, as usual, to ignore the chaos. I was about to simply roll into bed, quickly turn down the halogen lamp, and curl into a fitful sleep, in denial about the sorry state of my cluttered room. This time, though, I stopped myself and asked what I would do if I had a guest sleeping over. Instantly I knew the answer to that question. So I decided to experiment. I stuffed the dirty clothes in the hamper. Threw away the *Times*. Made the bed. Lit my yellow Museum of Modern Art vase-sized candle, and some incense as well. Turned the light down to an amber glow. Prepared a cup of warm milk sprinkled with nutmeg and cinnamon. Put on a CD of Franz Liszt's late piano pieces. Eventually I drifted off into a cloud of sleep much deeper than any I would have experienced if I'd simply left the mess to take care of itself. Perhaps without fully realizing its implications at the time, I was now having my first date with the Boyfriend Within.

I soon realized from chatting around, though, that this nifty concept of the Boyfriend Within was vulnerable to all sorts of misinterpretation. At its jokiest it could sound like the title of a manual for one-handed entertainment. At its worst, like a sermon on the joys of narcissism and self-love, a sort of New Age revisiting of Ayn Rand on "the virtue of selfishness." It could be interpreted as adult nostalgia for the secret companion of our childhood, the imaginary friend we spoke to when our actual friends were too much trouble. And it, of course, brings to mind the prescription to get in touch with "the Child Within" that's already current in our culture. Put "the Child Within" together with gay romance and you end up with something that could sound like the platform of the National Association for Man-Boy Love.

"The Boyfriend Within's really about taking care of the little boy inside you, right?" a friend asked. Well, yes and no. The problem with such interpretations is that they tend to be pat generalizations or name brands meant to apply to everyone. As I came to discover gradually, the Boyfriend Within is made of qualities we find attractive in ourselves but often imagine others to possess more fully, as well as of dormant qualities we wish to nurture and grow. Either way, each person's cluster of qualities is unique and peculiar to them, and, like all of us, is always changing and evolving as well. The Boyfriend Within isn't some high concept, after all. He's part of yourself.

So there's more to meeting the Boyfriend Within than mere wishful thinking, or philosophizing. About a week after my initial sleepover with the Boyfriend Within, I designed a practical technique, a *Procedure* for keeping him steadily and reliably in my life. Exasperated with reading a cacophony of self-help books and trying to apply them to my particular pain, I simply sat down one day with a pad and felt-tip pen and started asking some basic questions about my life. You know the sort: Why am I sitting home alone on a sunny Sunday? Why do all my close relationships backfire? When will love come my way? But this time, I waited for the answers. Not from some channeled spirit, but from a self-reliant source of wisdom and strength within. Slowly I began to "hear" answers and to write them down. For some reason, I felt moved to write down the answers with a pen different from the one used to write the original questions—in the spirit of those gestalt psychology exercises where you switch seats to talk to different sides of yourself.

It was this Voice I "heard" that led me to get more

in touch with that part of myself I've come to think of as the Boyfriend Within. A well-known author once advised me on the subject of boyfriends: "You're the only person who knows what you really need from a lover. Don't be influenced by anyone else on this. Listen to yourself. You may be surprised." The same is true with the Voice and with the Boyfriend Within. Along the way in this book you'll be hearing some of the answers the Voice made to me. Hopefully they'll be informative. But more important, you'll be guided soon on how to use a *Procedure* with two pens and a pad of paper to get in touch with your own Voice, which could be thought of as the Voice of the Boyfriend Within, generously sharing his wisdom with you, as any good boyfriend would. I'm convinced everyone has this power. That everyone's Boyfriend Within is unique, personal. That the Boyfriend Within and the Voice go mysteriously hand in hand. (As we became more familiar, I even began thinking of the Boyfriend Within as my BFW, or Inner B.)

In the months following my forty-fifth birthday, as the curve of my romantic and sexual activity declined as precipitously as the Dow Jones in a bear market, the curve of my contacts with the Boyfriend Within began to rise. The helpful Voice gradually became an ordinary part of my life—a garden-variety voice that offered opinions on daily questions about life, love, and where to go on vacation. I didn't need communiqués from angels. I just needed to sit down and focus. I just needed a pad and pens. I was anxious to figure out some of the burning questions of my life with the newfound help of the Boyfriend Within.

I'm convinced that listening with the inner ear is a talent anyone can cultivate. Everyone has a guiding Voice within. When it is located, good results are indicated. Certainly it's made changes for the better in my life. These changes speeded up when I could locate the Voice and the Boyfriend Within as surely as I could locate the mood I think of as "The Middle of the Night"—the mood of panic about being alone, or being yesterday's news, or believing that the agent from L.A. had a point. By building a daily, casual relationship with the Boyfriend Within, I didn't escape these moods, nor did I escape true setbacks and bad times. But I began to see upsetting tremors as early warning signs, as opportunities to consult the inner compass and take direction from there. It isn't so much that my circumstances have changed, or that great fame, money, and success have come my way, but just that my attitude toward the usual stuff has been transmogrified in a completely positive way. Life with the Boyfriend Within hasn't become unrecognizably different, just smoother, warmer, and more focused and clear.

That's how this book came to be, a book I certainly never thought I'd be writing. I decided to follow my hunch and look for the Boyfriend Within.

This is what I found.

THE PROCEDURE
FOR FINDING THE VOICE

Sit down at a table with a tablet
of paper and two felt-tip pens. I always
sit on a folding wooden chair at my
small, square kitchen table.
Whatever spot you choose,
it helps to return to the same place.

I began one day when I got
really frustrated. All the therapy and
meditating and yoga weren't enough.
And I'd had lots of the above.
I felt I had to make an effort to figure
out some questions and answers for myself.
I'd hit bottom, which you usually need to hit
before you can rise again to the surface,
and which reminds you that these problems
must finally be faced by you and you alone.
All the advice in the world won't help
unless you've found your own balance first.
My persistent pain was like an endlessly
ringing telephone. When I picked up a pen

to jot down questions, it was like picking up the
    telephone.
All I had to do was say, Hello?
The Voice was on the other end with answers.

At first, in the early, scattershot days, I wrote down
    lots of questions.
I did it just to get in the mood, to get to know the
    Voice,
to hear its answers,
and to get some sense of where
we were going together. That's why two pens:
a pen for me, a pen for the Voice.
In a way, all I was doing was writing
down my most private thoughts.
But it was more than that. I know myself.
And I know that the Voice and I are not exactly the
    same.
I wish it were me. But it's not.
I can be diffident, shy, guarded, arrogant.
The Voice is always friendly and generous.
The Voice doesn't have a shell around it.

I always felt quite good after those sessions.
I know they helped me.
This book is a record of those Q&As

and of my attempts to figure out what they meant:
It's definitely a Procedure *anyone can try at home.*
You should keep a record too. You might think of
this book as more of a compass than a map.
My answers can only point toward your own.

CHAPTER ONE

QUESTION: *Why don't I have a boyfriend?*
THE VOICE: *I don't know.*

As SUGGESTED IN the *Procedure,* for a week

or so I experimented, warming up by writing

down quick, spontaneous questions addressing

the crises of the moment—"What's wrong?" or

"How am I going to get through tonight?" or

"Should I call him back?" When I asked, for instance, how I was going to get through the night, I wrote down the Voice's response as: "Only do whatever you feel like doing. And check back with me every hour." The directive was gladly taken, and it was fun. I ended up having a late-night snack of oysters at a place down the street with a friend. I was limbering up for the dialogue and the education that was about to begin.

One day I dove in and asked one of the questions at the heart of this whole enterprise: "Why don't I have a boyfriend?" No sense wasting time, I told myself neurotically. Now, some people beginning this process already have boyfriends, and their first significant question might be different, such as, quoting the old song, "Is that all there is?" But for me, and for many others I'm sure, this boyfriend question needs to be answered and cleared up before moving on. This chapter is concerned with just that necessary clearing, a kind of romantic spring cleaning. So imagine my disappointment when I sat down in earnest to begin to reach the Boyfriend Within, only to receive the reply noted above. Needless to say, "I don't know" didn't do much for me at first, except to disappoint and really annoy.

"Humph," I thought. "Some Oracle of Delphi!

Everyone else channels all these amazing, lyrical, poetic, wise voices from the beyond. They get guardians full of depth and dignity. I'm stuck with a slacker. Next thing I know he'll be calling me 'Dude' and shoving off on his skateboard. Just my luck." But it was my Voice, and I was stuck with it. What do you do when your Ouija board supplies only incoherent, garbled messages? Return it?

As I delved deeper, though, I felt nudged in a direction by the vagueness of the answer. Perhaps the Voice wasn't being so cool after all. Perhaps the Voice was even getting warm. There may be no final explanation for those of us without boyfriends, just guesses. We're bachelors or widowers or loners, whether temporarily or always, whether we've been left, or perhaps have set our standards a little too high, or haven't been on a date in a year, or live in a remote locale. The only exceptions are those who absolutely say, "I don't want a boyfriend." And they might not be open and flexible enough to tap into the Boyfriend Within anyway.

The other day, while cruising the Internet, I stopped at a cute guy's gif (graphic image) to which he'd attached the posted caveat: "Not looking for someone who wants to move in with me. Or who wants to be my boyfriend. Just someone who won't be

31

able to keep his hands off me." That was simple. He doesn't have a boyfriend because he doesn't want one. (If you believe his mixed message, that is.)

A prime cause for not having a boyfriend comes from tying oneself in psychological knots. One way I know to untie these knots is with a therapist. I've been in therapy for twenty years, on and off; with an Episcopalian nun-priest-therapist, no less. I love seeing her. Where else can I talk about myself for forty-five minutes? Dwell on my every twist and turn? And not have to be polite by trading off and listening to a friend? Or be afraid that the friend I'm talking to has ulterior motives and might secretly be saying what I want to hear, or might secretly want to pull me in or push me away? It's worth the money to have a neutral spot at which to debrief every week.

A friend told me recently of the "pattern" he'd "discovered" in therapy—though it had been perfectly evident to all of us around him since day one. He was guilty of dancing the notorious "cha-cha." It goes like this: He would become involved with someone. They'd quickly become boyfriends. After a few months, he'd start to feel restless, weird, angry, trapped. He'd move a few steps one way, then twist and go in another direction. He'd cause problems. Eventually the boyfriend would split. As soon as he'd split, my friend would want him back.

He'd send roses, call, show up with passes for press seats at a Calvin Klein fashion show. This stunt was pretty transparent.

Now, through therapy, he knows why he doesn't have a boyfriend, or at least why he *might* not. And luckily he knows what he can do about the situation. With work, he can become attuned to the alarms that warn of another crisis. When they go off next time, he can find the reflex within himself to remedy the situation. That way he'll have a boyfriend in bed with him, asleep, spooning, if he wants. Not necessarily, of course. But it's possible.

Like my friend with his classic "cha-cha" routine that gets in the way of meeting, falling in love, or staying together, everyone has insecurities that may lead to patterns of conflict and avoidance. Some people feel they're basically unlovable. Or that other people are unlovable. Some are control freaks. Some are afraid of being suffocated. Some confuse sex with love. Some confuse unavailability with attractiveness. Some prefer fireworks. Some are searching for Daddy. Some are running away from Daddy. And on and on it goes. As Annie Lennox put it: "Some people like to abuse you. Some people like to be abused."

•   •   •

ALONG the way to finding the Boyfriend Within, I've found it useful, besides contacting the Voice as outlined in the *Procedure,* to also do a series of "Awareness Exercises." These are close to the sorts of exercises you might do in therapy, or in self-discovery seminars. Some are designed to make us aware of patterns of thinking, feeling, or behaving that have contributed to unhappy habits in our lives. In sixties lingo, their purpose is "consciousness raising." Others are designed to help us develop new ways to contact and stay attuned to the BFW. These exercises can be quite practical: In one case, we'll be trying to dream up as many dates as possible with our Boyfriend Within. Or they can be more theoretical: In another case, we'll be listing repercussions of looking at the world as something other than a mail-order catalog from which to pick boyfriends. If relating to the Voice and the Boyfriend Within is the heart and soul of this book, the Awareness Exercises are its muscles and skeleton. Both are necessary.

You'll need only one pen to scratch down your responses in the Awareness Exercises, and you might want to keep a record of what you write—to look back on, to add to. These responses won't be as charged or unpredictable as the guiding or oblique pronouncements from a sometimes cryptic Voice. Unlike the Q&A format for contacting the Voice, they mostly involve list making. Doing these exercises, however, helps greatly in moving the process of finding the Boyfriend Within into fast-forward. There will be fifteen Awareness Exercises spread out throughout the book—taken together, they can point you in the right direction.

Awareness Exercise One

Write down a list of your own neurotic patterns. Once written out, these bumps in the night lose some of their power to control and alarm. They become demystified. The door is off their closet, so to speak. Exorcising, as we've learned from the movies, is always about naming the demon. So you can begin to exorcise these neurotic routines by putting them into words. Once you begin, you'll find other patterns occurring to you while you're walking down the street or driving in a car. Go back and add them to the list. Every time you identify one of these neurotic patterns, your emotional IQ will shoot up about five points. Here's my own list, and a few explanatory comments:

- I seem to be attracted to villains, to the sort of guy who plays pirates in movies.

Everyone else takes one look at him and thinks, "I don't trust that guy." I look at him and think, "Hmmmmm. . . ." A related type is the "gimbo" (a gay bimbo), whose muscles and physical desirability make him an attractive arm to want to hang on, regardless of any lack of depth. Whoever these gimbos really may be, I'm drawn to their potential as cartoon characters in the self-created comic strip of my love life.

• I'm sometimes drawn to people who seem at first capable of making my life easier.

They mother me. Or, more important, they father me by having the big bucks, buying dinner and theater tickets, and always paying for the cab. They have famous and influential friends to introduce me to. The problem is that eventually there's a price to be paid. And just as with a new credit card, the bill usually doesn't come for a couple of months. That's when the demands, and the uglier parts of their character I've chosen to overlook, become more glaring. And I find myself feeling like just a glorified gigolo. (This scenario, of course, worked better circa age twenty-two.)

• After a few weeks with anyone, my eye begins to wander.

I feel I'm missing something. I want to go
out, party, develop new tastes. I love romance
and the excitement of getting to know someone.
But after a while I begin to feel as if I'm back
home living with my parents, listening to them
argue, staying in at night doing homework under
duress. I don't like anything that reminds me too
much of the childhood blahs. As a result, I
quickly reconfigure my new beau as a prison
guard or truant officer or busybody.

Almost everyone can tally inner and outer explanations for their predicament in life. I've developed
quite a list of my neurotic patterns by making Awareness Exercise One a part of my regular mental routine.
A few days after making my original list, I suddenly
noticed that I *always* give my phone number but
never ask for the other guy's number in return. I'm
then left feeling either rejected, all-alone-by-the-tele-
phone style, or pursued. It's a self-imposed version of
the chador worn by Islamic women. I veil my desires.
My last boyfriend was perfect for my neuroses: He
could only be reached by voice mail—which meant he
was consistently distant, unavailable, and in control.

Of course, not everyone who doesn't have a
boyfriend has such obvious neurotic patterns to blame,

or to change—though to some extent we all have a few. In Awareness Exercise Two we'll be dealing with "environmental factors," which do affect everyone and which can have an impact on whether you're single or involved: age, location, death, sickness, career. (There *is* a real world out there, after all.) We can look at this situation in another context: Many people who wish to have a million dollars, don't. Is this just because they don't really want a million dollars? No, they typically have little if any control over the matter. Some live in North Korea. Some don't want to do the dirty deeds that might be required to make a million dollars, given their age and station and educational level. Some just don't have the tools. Some aren't in the right place at the right time. These are all examples of factors that are part of an environment and not entirely self-created.

I don't mean to belittle the homespun truth that anyone who really wants a mate can usually find one. Or that anyone who doesn't, whether consciously or un-, often doesn't really want one. Or to suggest that dark forces of the id aren't sometimes at work that need to be exposed and named and put to rest. But I also know that in the real world on which we stub our toe, shit happens. People grow older. There are differences in maturity: You just might not have the patience for an otherwise buff guy who continuously comes up with the-dog-ate-my-homework excuses, such as "My answering machine must have lost your message." As a friend reasonably complained, "It seems the saner I get, the fewer people there are to relate to."

Awareness Exercise Two

Write down the environmental factors involved in your not having a boyfriend. Not having met the right person is certainly an acceptable explanation. But there are others. Most people find this second list more surprising than the first. In this psychological era we've perhaps become more used to contemplating the navel of our feelings than smelling the coffee. Both aspects of experience need to be taken into account. Here are a few examples of my own environmental factors:

- AIDS
    Certainly, among gays, this disease has been an entirely unexpected meteor crashing into everyone's best-laid plans. I've experienced the special difficulties when two people of different HIV-status become romantically involved but feel *medically* uncomfortable with each other. Disease

and death are real, though. We didn't invent them.

- Career

I hate to admit that each one of my last three books has been written mostly during a bachelor phase. I'd rather say that they flourished like flowers in the nurturing sun of love. But it's not true. Selfish spans of uncompromising hours were incalculably helpful. Remember the quite honest line in *Philadelphia*, when Tom Hanks, playing a gay lawyer, admitted, "I love the law." People can love their jobs, love success. Perhaps for them it's not the moment for romance. Give them a few years. To everything there is a season.

- Not having met the right person

Sure, there's *someone* for everyone. But who wants just someone? Unless you want a boyfriend the way you want a Jag or a Range Rover, for image and kicks, you might want to hold out. For me, the prospect of a boyfriend has to compete with a quality of life that's already set, and at least pretty satisfactory. As in one of the worn clichés of on-line profiles on AOL: "I'm looking for Mr. Right, not Mr. Right Now."

And then there are those who simply aren't being honest with themselves. These types love to join in the complaining circle at dinner, moaning about being boyfriendless, but truth is, they just don't want a boyfriend. On an unwritten, probably unconscious ledger sheet they've already added up the pluses of a boyfriend versus the minuses. The minus column has secretly won out as the more compelling to them.

Awareness Exercise Three

List the pluses and minuses in having a boyfriend. To find out what you're really thinking, draw a line down the middle of a blank sheet of paper, listing on one side the pluses of having a boyfriend, and on the other, the minuses. See how the columns add up. One side might prove stronger than the other because of a longer list of entries, or because of the undeniable draw of a few concerns of most importance to you. Both quality and quantity need to be weighed in this decision. Maybe you'll discover the Boyfriend Within is the terminus on your particular route, the truly preferred destination. Why waste the effort pretending to look for a boyfriend if you're really ambivalent?

On the plus side, I'm attracted by the advantages of:

41

- Intimacy
- Division of labor
- Nursing
- Sleeping together
- Buying real estate together

On the minus side of my ledger sheet, I find that I'm certainly put off by:

- Snoring
- Having to report in
- Enduring a doubled number of obligatory parties and dinners

In my own case, the plus side wins out because of both the quality and quantity of the positive items listed.

WHETHER being single has been subconsciously chosen, or is a matter of circumstance, or has been selected with eyes clear and unblinking, I find there's often, maybe even relentlessly, a stigma in our postliberated era to not having a boyfriend. This stigma can manifest itself as a pointed finger accusing one of crimes such as an "intimacy problem!" Notice, next time, that everyone who uses such clunky terms hasn't necessarily paid the tuition, or put in the study time, to get the advanced degrees in counseling and psychology to license them to use such jargon. They're talking the talk without having walked the walk. The unfortunate, and frequent, assumption behind these comments is that people who aren't coupled are lemons, defectives, emotional squirts.

When Howard and I were having our truly screwy, though wonderful, time together, friends, especially distant ones, would look at us with dewy eyes as though we were somehow to be emulated. "If only I were you, I'd be happy," their goo-goo faces seemed to say. "If only you knew," I always thought (humorously) in return. I loved Howard. I was happy with him most days. But somehow our brand of love and happiness wasn't the item these friends' eyes told me they were in the market for. Now that I'm boyfriend-less, I get lots of looks and comments that tell me just the opposite of what they said before. "I'm sorry you're a Tin Man, missing a heart," they seem to be saying. Like Judy Collins, I've looked at life from both sides now. Or, more accurately perhaps, life's looked at me from both sides now.

Pondering these matters, I gradually learned to make room for the Voice's answer: "I don't know."

There is a place, too, for my therapist's answers. And maybe there's even a place for the Hollywood agent's skepticism. But deep in the heart of the Voice's slacker reply is a nonjudgmental, haunting tone that is not only celestine and hip and trendy, but may be more respectful of the way things are, the way people are.

Recently, when I was getting a haircut, my barber said, quoting *his* therapist: "The reason you're on earth is to experience life. That's it. Everything else, including whether you get love or money, is just icing." I don't know if the Voice was exactly saying *that*. But he (why not she? why not it? I'll have to get back to that question) . . . he was saying something similar.

It's worthwhile hedging your bets, though, by continuing to work at the question of why you do what you do. Take time every day to revisit selected Awareness Exercises from this chapter and those to come. Really get in there and dig out the blackened weeds deeply rooted in your own soil. But I'd caution you that one session of self-examination a day is plenty, and remember it's for yourself and should be done alone. It's certainly not something real boyfriends need to do together—perform surgery on each other's psyches. They just need to love each other. And that's not territory you need to overdo with your Boyfriend Within, either—as you gradually begin to know him and court him and love him.

I can't believe how many times I've had this maddening "Why don't I have a boyfriend?" conversation recently. The next time you find yourself having this conversation with someone—and if you're caught reading this book, chances are you will—try taking on some of the attitude of the Voice. It's okay to say, "I don't know," because you must admit finally that you don't know everything about anyone, not even yourself. So maybe say: "I don't know why I don't have a boyfriend, and I don't know why you don't have a boyfriend. We may never know. You may someday. Or you may never. But *I* think you're boyfriend material." Or just throw civility to the winds and kiss him on the lips, or hold his hand, or touch him, or stroke his back, or at least smile . . . something. You'll probably like yourself better as a sympathetic know-nothing anyway than as a correct know-it-all. I found "I don't know" to be a useful mantra in many situations. And more often than not, truthful: "I don't know."

Incidentally, as someone who's been in boyfriend heaven, I can tell you that there comes a time when even boyfriends would do well to discover the Boyfriend Within. I watched my relationship with Howard go from loneliness to fudgy togetherness to a kind of aloneness again: that is, the two of us sitting peacefully in the same room—reading, say—but thrown back on our own resources. That's a phase of coming down to earth that other coupled friends of mine have corroborated as being their experience as well. It could be that between lovers the prescription for the Boyfriend Within might become a fandango, a recipe for a threeway, or even a fourway. Anyway, many boyfriends within and without! I'm losing count.

I think, too, about gay teenagers. I never had a huge mess of a problem with coming out. I went to Columbia College in the 1970s. Even though I hadn't had sex with a boy since my friend Bobby, when I was thirteen, I just marched down to the Gay Lounge, met the president of the gay student group, who took me to meet the dean of housing, who was also gay, and I ended up with a great room in Furnald Hall. Talk about positive reinforcement! But if I'd known about the Boyfriend Within when I was pining after the blond basketball player I had a crush on in junior high, I might have had a less miserable, if no less frustrated, adolescence. Not to mention having somewhere to go with my big secret of being gay—I did manage to keep this secret, or thought I did, all through high school. I know that many gay teenagers today still are troubled (and too many become hopeless and commit suicide). If they find their Boyfriend Within, they'll at least have someone or something to tide them over until they get out of Iowa or the Panhandle, and perhaps they'll have invaluable practice early on in the ways of adult love. They might even feel better about life and themselves.

And what about women? I hear my women friends discussing this topic even more than my gay friends—if that's possible. Certainly, with divorces on the rise, many people of all sexual persuasions are finding a new need to become acquainted with the Boyfriend/Girlfriend Within. My straight trainer hasn't had much luck looking for a Girlfriend Without after his last, who put up with him for about three years. Between dumbbell sets, I tried out a variation of the concept on him. "Maybe you should get in touch with the Girlfriend Within." I suggested. "Would that make me a lesbian?" he asked. I didn't have an answer. Though I guess the Girlfriend Within brings together straight men and lesbians in a way I hadn't considered before. They might both be looking for the Girlfriend Within. But that's just too confusing. I'm losing count again.

I think that finding the Boyfriend Within—or the Girlfriend Within—as in finding the Boyfriend Without: that real, 3-D boyfriend, can be a path toward greater realization, or what is called dharma in Buddhism. The idea of dharma, as I understand it from some popular American version of Buddhism that's been filtered down from college courses and pop-psych books and Allen Ginsberg and Hermann Hesse and Keanu Reeves in *Little Buddha,* is that you can follow a path of service, or a path of religious devotion, or a path of mental or even physical discipline, and eventually arrive wiser and happier, and at the same spot as those on other paths. The point is to choose a path and stick with it, stick with *anything* that's not hurtful. Your consistent focus may release a force that will unpack lessons along the way: different ways, same lessons. I don't know why a path of romantic love couldn't do the same. It seems so much more up the alley of everyone I know. I've been on it—with occasional detours down its sexual side-paths—for some time. And now here I am at an intersection. I can at least corroborate that there is change and growth and help and some happiness to be had on such a path. Enlightenment, though, I don't know. There it is again: *I don't know.*

AWARENESS EXERCISES:

1. List neurotic patterns that might be getting in the way of your meeting, getting to know, or learning to happily live with a boyfriend.

2. List environmental factors that may in part explain any difficulties you are experiencing in meeting, getting to know, or living with a boyfriend.

3. Draw a line down the middle of a blank sheet of paper. On one side, list the pluses of having a boyfriend. On the other side, list the minuses. See how your own personal ledger sheet balances out.

CHAPTER TWO

QUESTION: *Who is the Boyfriend Within?*

THE VOICE: *Well, in your case, he's definitely your "better half."*

By THE TIME the above exchange came about with my Voice, I'd grown used to his sarcasm. It turns out that my particular Voice has quite a sense of humor. More than I do, certainly, or at least more than I usually allow to seep into my writing. Getting acquainted with the Voice has already added something new and positive to my life. Of course, not everyone might consider sarcasm a boon. But I did. I realized that much of my problem with self-help wisdom has always been the vapid, smug, air-conditioned tone of voice in which so much of it is delivered. The contents are fine. But the package is too often a matter of Hallmark Greeting Card meets Suspiciously Blissful Cult Member. I'm glad my Voice has some bite. You may have found some refreshing, surprising qualities in your own Voice by now as well. If you haven't, be patient. You may, gradually.

Thankfully this time the Voice's answer to my query wasn't so cryptic as his "I don't know" of chapter 1. Flip, yes. Cryptic, no. I knew immediately just what he was poking at. He was poking at the burning personal issue I always associate with Romans 7:15 in the New Testament. That's where Saint Paul, sounding dangerously, at least at first blush, like a nut case, cries out: "I cannot even understand my own actions. I do not do what I want to do but what I hate." Now, Saint Paul—with his Epistle to the Romans, his other epistles, and his reputation as the man responsible for some of the favorite quotations used by self-righteous preachers when they want to put down homosexuality—has never been one of my heroes. Even Romans 7:15 could sound like a puritan argument against the desires of the flesh. And it may well be. You know the drill: Anything that feels good is bad. Anything that requires self-discipline or self-denial is good. Gays define themselves at least in part by their willingness to act on their sexuality and hormonal drives. They want satisfaction. They gotta be them and be accepted and be happy as well. Ergo gays must be bad.

Needless to say that wasn't my association when this particular verse became one of my mantras during my forty-fifth year of grasping at any seemly explanation floating by. But I did feel that I needed rewiring. My romantic life and loves had blown enough fuses in the past decade that I was beginning to wonder. I felt as if I were shorted out somehow. As if the wires of my life had been crossed, as if a white wire had been connected to a black wire, and a black wire to a white. The result was that love and romance too often became associated with bad feelings, bad choices in partners, and general emotional power outages.

Take Dirk. One morning, during week two of a liaison that went on for almost a year, we had just rolled out of bed. I was brewing coffee. Dirk, wearing my green plaid Brooks Brothers bathrobe, dialed the phone while sitting across from me on the couch. He

explained without flinching to his unnamed inter-
locutor: "I'm in the phone booth on the train coming
in from Long Island. I'll be at Penn Station in a half
hour." He then strolled off nonchalantly to shower
and shave. Whenever I tell this story, everyone hoots
and hollers at my naïveté. Why didn't I say anything?
Wasn't that a glaring tip-off that something was wrong
with this picture? At the time, though, I blocked my
response. Dirk rewarded my acceptance of his unusual
behavior by telling me more of what I wanted to hear.
"I'm the one you've been praying would come your
way," he once bragged. He made claims that perhaps
only a Boyfriend Within could truly satisfy—that he
was going to make me happy, secure, and loved forever. In return, I spliced the white wire of my love and
affection to the black wire of his evidently sociopathic
personality.

A woman friend of mine, Gini, was seeing a self-
made millionaire from Los Angeles who'd recently
separated from his wife. He had a habit of getting off
the phone in a manner that would leave her somehow terminally off the hook as well. Once he was
calling from his cell phone while driving on the free-
way. "I'm going through a tunnel, I'm losing you, I'll
call you back at the other end," he said, his voice carried away in the gust of an electronic dust storm. He

didn't call back. She actually worried that he'd been involved in an accident. She left several messages on his cell phone voice mail. No reply. In those early days, the two had no mutual friends, and she half believed that she'd lost him in some horrible pileup. When he called back ten days later, he was entirely relaxed and oblivious. "I've been in Hawaii, why?" he responded to her startled question about his whereabouts.

One Saturday night I went with my friend Mike to G, a gay bar in Manhattan's Chelsea district that looks like a Banana Republic store filled with Banana Republic–style models from their latest ad campaign. We sat next to each other on a banquette to watch the show. Nearby a cute, generically Italian-looking guy—dashing dark eyes, dark eyebrows, five o'clock shadow—sat hunkered on a hassock behind his boyfriend, who was perched in front of him. He kept one arm around his boyfriend's chest, feeling him up nonstop while beaming stares at Mike. When we began to leave, the romancer with a modular personality rubbed Mike's leg as he walked by while continuing to fondle his boyfriend's pecs. When I told another friend a few days later about this triangular incident, he said casually, "Oh, I know him." As proof, he described not only the guy but the same incident, with himself as the third point of the triangle. "Now there's a *real* man for you," he joked.

I tell these stories because they each provide examples of crossed wires, of going for drama rather than substance, of what happens when good people feel drawn to "bad news." I liked Dirk all the more because he kept me on pins and needles. Without the slings and arrows of uncertainty piercing me every so often, I would have been content to look at the two of us disappointingly sitting in my apartment without much to say to each other. With all the startling lies, I became too distracted to notice. I mistook mystery for true interest. Similarly, Gini's entrepreneur learned that he could count on her to take his calls. If she didn't, who knew when the next opportunity might come, or when the battery might go dead in his cellular phone midsentence. The gigolo at G instinctively understood the theatricality and power of unsettling triangular intrigue.

The best depiction I know of a character with just such crossed wires can be found in my favorite rental video, Alfred Hitchcock's *Vertigo*, where Jimmy Stewart plays Johnny, an ex-detective plagued with vertigo who chooses dizzying romance over reliable affection—with disastrous results. The woman drawing him into a doomed drama is Judy/Melanie, played as both ice princess and cheesy salesgirl by Kim Novak. You may remember her in high heels and couture dress, navigating madly up the right angles of the vertiginous wooden stairs of the bell tower of a Spanish mission outside San Francisco. But the character who haunts the movie—and me—is Midge (played by Barbara Bel Geddes). She's the lingerie designer who's there unconditionally for Johnny, waiting to pour his scotch, steer him to his next lead, and visit him in the sanitarium to help pick up the pieces of his life after he cracks up. Depicted as the sort of 1950s reliable good girl whom men wouldn't bother to make passes at, she's the very heart of nurturing love. And, of course, she hardly registers as a blip on Johnny's malfunctioning psychic screen.

Yet Midge seems perfect to me as my Boyfriend Within—allowing for some gender bending from central casting. For in her direction lie sanity, peace, happiness. Of course, if Johnny had gone for Midge there wouldn't have been a movie. And it's a given that we all like a little drama in our lives, and a few exciting plot twists. It's exciting to have our hot buttons pushed. But one way to describe the change that began happening in me when I got in touch with the Boyfriend Within was that I made some room in my life as well for Midge's contribution.

My purpose, though, isn't to lay my Boyfriend Within on you. You have to find your own. And everyone's has a slightly different constitution. For instance, I have friend—two male, two female—for whom creativity rather than intimacy is the Big Issue. They really do seem to have paintings and pop songs and novels and movies in preproduction within them. Yet they have a creative block about allowing themselves to do the necessary painting, or piano playing, or automatic writing that would let their particular genie out of his bottle. Three of them trace their stopped corks back to childhood repression; one dismisses such explanations as corny. In each of their cases I have a hunch that they'd find their Boyfriend Within to be quite a creative spirit. If mine is Midge, theirs may be Jackson Pollock, the abstract expressionist artist with apparently boundless energy and a savage, primitively inchoate desire to reinvent the wheel of art history.

For these friends, ignoring their Boyfriend Within is tantamount to denying their own creativity. They have trouble admitting that the little snatches of a tune that come to them in the middle of the night, or the great opening image they envision for a movie, or the urge to merge colors on a flat surface, really matter. They tend to think that such necessities of life for the creative person are really just luxuries reserved for someone else—for Michelangelo, or Wolfgang Amadeus Mozart. While my dates with the Boyfriend Within tend to be much quieter, more nurturing, and stress free than other appointments in my life, theirs could be high-energy opportunities to express themselves.

Another acquaintance has such a creative green thumb that he can turn any weed into a beanstalk. Creativity isn't his problem. He moves into a bleak studio apartment in a tenement on Avenue A and two weeks later it's been transformed into a magical pashadom. He's usually content to stay there and simply be the nice guy he is. For this poet of everyday life, though, the Big Issue is networking, selling himself, getting out of a flat job as a receptionist at Potholder, Inc., where he isn't utilizing his many talents.

My creative friend may actually be uneasy about getting in touch with the driving Tony Robbins within—the part of himself filled with all the testosterone required to do business in pushy America. I think of Tony Robbins because of his late-night infomercials promising money, success, and happiness for the price of a set of his *Personal Power* audiotapes about channeling positive thinking into positive results. While the medium in which he peps us up with his big hair and big teeth might be off-putting to some, his message of the virtues of pursuing personal happiness is as old and as exhilarating as the Declaration of Independence. For my friend on Avenue A, his dates with his Boyfriend Within might be filled with making lists to focus his ambition and plot the steps: a five-month plan, a five-year plan, a fifty-year mission statement. His Boyfriend Within may actually resemble one of those moguls photographed by Annie Leibovitz for *Vanity Fair* at the annual Allen & Co. summer retreat in Sun Valley, Idaho: all tan, all business, all drive.

Whether your Boyfriend Within is more Midge or Jackson Pollock, or Tony Robbins, though, you can be sure of one thing: He's also part you. He's your chance to become more comfortable with uncharted territory that's been inside you all along. He's there to help you rewire yourself. Of course, rewiring can be an intense activity. That's why I usually only spend somewhere between a half hour and two hours at a stretch with my Boyfriend Within, engaging in some of the activities I'll be discussing in the next chapter. But during that time I get a chance to be in a relationship that doesn't involve head games, or self-destructive fantasies, or pins and needles. These are trial runs with health and happiness, or creativity and power, or peace and love. Who knows? With practice, a half hour with your Boyfriend Within today might develop into an hour tomorrow.

LOOKING for the Boyfriend Within begins much like looking for a Boyfriend Without—that real boyfriend somewhere out there in the world. There's a certain amount of taking stock that transpires. I remember reading a book I picked up at someone's summer house. Its title was *How to Marry the Man of Your Choice.* Its middle-aged author presented her dates as job interviews. She'd ask pointed questions of these prospective partners, questions designed to x-ray their character. She'd distinguish the different signals and clues dropped by these men that would point her toward her final decision. When she found a man who closely matched the blueprint of desire in her head, she'd design an agenda to move him toward a ride-into-the-sunset conclusion. Her book jacket contained a piece of information more powerful than any blurb: She'd married the man of her choice and was happy.

The persona of this author made me uncomfortable, though. She seemed a consciousness-raised revamping of the old archetype of the wily, seductive, entrapping female. I wondered if she'd ever found *her* Boyfriend Within. Yet her businesslike approach to matters of the heart did appeal to me. In searching for a closer relationship with my Boyfriend Within, I've certainly had to do a lot of analyzing, temperature taking, and list making as well. Love—whether inner or outer—seems to go hand in hand with work.

When I begin thinking about my Boyfriend Within, I always recognize first that I'm really caught somewhere between the lure of the shopping mall of boyfriend hunting and my own inner tugs toward peace and contentment, the realm of the Boyfriend Within. That is, I'm oriented at least as much outwardly as inwardly. I resist a bit. One amusing way to try to ease into a true encounter with the Boyfriend Within is not to resist at all but to give in briefly to the savor of thinking romantically—by seeing ourselves as a player in the world, or as a contestant on *The Dating Game.* If we're spirits, we're spirits in bodies, or, as Sting put it, "spirits in a material world." I promise it's only a half step from here to slipping under the wave and becoming one with your rewarding Boyfriend Within.

The next Awareness Exercise will allow us to take a cool look at ourselves as "packages"—to go on an imaginary date with ourselves and size ourselves up.

People usually come away from this exercise happier than you might expect. They're not necessarily left feeling entirely objectified at all. Often they're surprised at how much they have to offer even in the most superficial of ways: pretty face, good bod, cool clothes.

Awareness Exercise Four

Write down what might make you desirable as a companion on the open market of dating and romance. You don't even have to look at yourself with any particular sensitivity, education, insight, or moral compass. When we look at ourselves through the cocked, calibrating eyes of someone slightly less sensitive and evolved than we assume ourselves to be, what do we see? Make a list of the most attractive qualities of the "package" that is you.

Looking for the positive from the point of view of an interested party, you might be surprised at all of the pluses you'd forgotten you had, of all the wrapped gifts lying under your particular tree. Everyone has something to offer. If you don't succeed in identifying your selling points at first, keep trying. It's a cheap level of self-awareness we're going for here. If nothing else, this exercise will get you used to accentuating the positive, and the Boyfriend Within will be nothing if not positive. Among the pleasures I found I could offer at least by proxy to my imaginary appraiser were:

- A buff, toned body

  I've been going to the gym ever since I was in college. I am not now nor have I ever been a physique magazine model. But I see my trainer twice a week. I swim fifteen laps twice a week. I ride the StairMaster for forty-five minutes while catching up on the week's magazines. When matters had grown too blubbery, I did what the mirror told me and went on a diet of 1500 calories a day for a couple of months. I blush to admit it, but now I could imagine going to bed with myself—at least for the sleeping part.

- My SoHo apartment

  For ten years I lived in Hell's Kitchen in Manhattan in an apartment that looked like a cross between an eternal graduate student's and a hustler's pad. "I feel like I should leave money on the kitchen table when I walk out," one friend said snidely. Then my current apartment on the top floor of an 1839 townhouse became available. The floor planks are wide. The back windows look out on tall trees. A fireplace is a welcome fixture, even if it doesn't work. "Nice apartment," people usually say when they stop by. I'd never heard that comment during my entire ten years in Hell's Kitchen. This apartment feels as atmospheric as Thoreau's cabin. Anyone who hangs out with me at home gets to spend time in my poetic cabin as well.

- A career

    The state university where I teach was generous enough to grant me tenure, and I use their Olympic-size swimming pool regularly. I've published books, magazine articles, and I'm writing a screenplay. These projects give me extra pocket money for going out to dinner, buying a Valentino suit, or taking weekend trips to inns in Vermont during leaf-peeping season. There's a feeling of accomplishment that any buddies of mine can share without even having to do the work. I've already done that part.

I've tested this Awareness Exercise on willing friends, asking for their claims to winning-contestant status. Mysteriously topping one friend's list was "my washer and dryer." Another bragged of his "extensive CD collection." A third made reference to his sexual prowess. "Blond" came up. Someone did complain, however: "I had to stop," he e-mailed me. "It was actually a strange reaction I had—as if I really didn't want to see myself objectively. Not so much because I was afraid of what I'd discover as the fact that if you never have a really clear handle on it, you can still fudge so much. . . . Verrry interesting."

The antidote to my friend's anxiety and frazzle can come from the Boyfriend Within. Just as any uneasy feelings brought up by doing the fourth Awareness Exercise can be alleviated by moving on to the fifth, designed to put us in touch with our inner qualities rather than trying to put a price tag on what we feel to be so obviously priceless. Hold onto any sensations of relief, or settling, or increased seriousness and maturity you might experience in passing between these exercises. For these are the very qualities of spirit you will be nurturing in yourself by turning further and further within.

Awareness Exercise Five

Now take a deep breath and make a list of your own most attractive inner qualities. You can replace the crass bruiser looking for a one-night stand projected in the last Awareness Exercise with someone who really cares about you, someone with depth and character.

Try to gauge which of your own personality traits would be most appealing to such a mature and discerning type. You won't discover the Boyfriend Within by doing Awareness Exercise Four. But in now writing down with clear-eyed honesty your own most attractive inner qualities, you're beginning to describe your Boyfriend Within. You're getting to know him.

This Awareness Exercise is perhaps the most valuable in the entire book. For here you actually meet your Boyfriend Within for the first time. It's like that first glimpse of a special someone across a crowded room. Some have reported seeing a glow around a stranger who went on to become special in their lives. Others can remember exactly what he was wearing, or what song was playing on the jukebox. There's the old cliché about hearing bells. Mostly, though, the importance of a new friend only becomes apparent over time, and we retrospectively color the original event to fit later events. Either way, you have to begin somewhere.

In doing this exercise, I created a longer list than usual, and one that built gradually over time. Perhaps I have a particularly healthy ego. When I asked my mother once why I was an only child, she lied, obviously, and said, "Because you were so perfect, we didn't want to push our luck." I believed her lie, and the remark forever colored my self-image, for better or worse. I think, though, that everyone can eventually come up with a list of their own positive inner qualities—those attributes that would attract them to themselves in the best of all possible circumstances. My list was:

- Sensitivity
- Self-esteem
- Sophistication
- Playfulness
- Focus
- Honesty

I don't need to spell out exhaustively the evidence I found for each of these, or all of their meanings peculiar to myself. Writing down one abstract word might not seem like much, but the words resonate with feelings that we want to grow and to live with more consistently. In Awareness Exercise Four, I derived pleasure from noticing that my developed shoulders were as sturdy as a wooden coat hanger. But I derived even more pleasure from Exercise Five by feeling the settled quality of "self-esteem," or the clear uprightness of "honesty," or the sober early-morning awakening of "focus."

This list is definitely important enough to spend some time with—both in the making and in the expanding. You might begin, as I did, with five or six characteristics, but you should continue to add to the list as you recognize more and more of these qualities within. Write them on a card small enough to fit in your wallet or pocket. Look at the card every so often. Add to it. The more familiar you become with spotting these qualities, the more familiar you become with your Boyfriend Within. You're strengthening him.

Awareness Exercise Six

For those who wish to go even further, though, there's this sixth Awareness Exercise, where you begin to write down those qualities you'd *like* to develop in the Boyfriend Within that perhaps are still dormant, faint, wishful. The divergence in different people's lists—as in different people—becomes obvious at this juncture. My list for Awareness Exercise Five constituted a fine compilation of attractive qualities. Some people shared, or might wish they shared, a few of these. But others' lists were filled with other qualities. Some I never thought about and don't particularly covet. ("Modesty," for instance, shows up on some people's lists, but not on mine.) But a few of the qualities of other people's Boyfriends Within I would very much like to have. In this case, though, you don't have to go cruising for someone new as a salve for your frustration or disappointment. You don't have to wish someone else's estimable boyfriend was yours. He's yours for the creating.

Write down those qualities you wish to develop in your Boyfriend Within. Be a genetic scientist. Think how you could rewrite the DNA code of your Boyfriend Within. My own wish list includes:

- Flexibility
- Emotional Expressiveness
- Warmth
- Generosity
- Loyalty
- Listening

By placing the two lists side by side, I could immediately see that my Boyfriend Within was more developed in areas of mind and character (sophistication, focus), and less developed in heart and soul (emotional expressiveness, generosity). By having devised my wish list of attributes I desired in my BFW, and underlining with emphasis my desire for a little more warmth and human kindness from him, I began to feel results. It was Pavlovian in a way, but this time I was both the dinner bell and the salivating dog.

When finished, copy down your list of inner qualities still in development on the flip side of the card filled with the list of qualities you already possess. Memorize both; refer to them. Some Post-its, with reminders such as "Flexibility," "Listening," "Discipline," or "Positive Thinking," could be helpful if stuck in key spots—on the refrigerator, next to the phone. Recognize as well all the incidents life will send your way to test these qualities. If you're nurturing generosity, you might not whisk by the guy holding open the post office door for you as he extends a paper cup for loose change. If it's listening you're trying to cultivate, you might notice the next time your mind wanders when your best friend is discussing a crucial career move he's contemplating.

I REMEMBER the Buddha being quoted as saying something to the effect that, "The hardest thing for human beings to give up is their suffering." I think that's true. We're attached to the causes of our suffering like kids to video games. We can't get enough. We invent new and better ways to suffer all the time—in sex, in work, in friendships, through technology. Learning to stop loving the bomb is a tall order and beyond my scope or that of this book. But by learning to rest awhile with the Boyfriend Within, we're actually viscerally giving up suffering for however long our sessions last. The hardest thing is weirdly among the simplest to pull off, at least for a few minutes at a time. As the poet Frank O'Hara put it: "Happiness / the least and best of human attainments." Luckily this happiness is gradually addicting.

Awareness Exercises:

4. List the most attractive qualities of the "package" that is you.
5. List your most attractive inner qualities.
6. List those qualities you want to more fully develop in your Boyfriend Within.

CHAPTER THREE

QUESTION: *How do I get to know the Boyfriend Within?*

THE VOICE: *To get to know the Boyfriend Within, you have to get outside yourself.*

INSTEAD OF ASKING and answering lots of introspective questions in this chapter, we'll be concentrating on the simple task of learning to date the Boyfriend Within. The chapter will consist of one extended and extensive Awareness Exercise—Awareness Exercise Seven. It's all about going "out" with your Boyfriend Within, the possibilities for which are limited only by your imagination and the desires and needs of your Boyfriend Within. Admittedly, though, this notion of dating takes some getting used to.

When planning dates with the Boyfriend Within, I always begin by sitting down to consider the possibilities. Do I feel like going to the movies? Eating in? Taking a walk? Going shopping? The point is that you need to schedule time with your Boyfriend Within just as consciously and intently as you would with a Boyfriend Without, or a business associate, or a new infatuation, or a cousin visiting from out of town. In this case, however, you won't need to compromise. So there will be no excuses for not having a pleasant time. You're free to do exactly what you feel like doing at the moment. And you're free to change plans on a dime. Just be careful not to cancel too often, or your Boyfriend Within might feel taken for granted or less important than any passing stranger.

I had a funny conversation recently with a friend on the topic of inner dates. He asked (sarcastically?) what kind of music my Boyfriend Within liked to listen to when we got together. I told him about some early twentieth-century French piano music we appreciated, and a Vivaldi "Gloria." "So he doesn't like the headbanger stuff?" my friend asked, knowingly referring to my occasional penchant for listening to English punk-rock bands or Satanic heavy metal when I'm in a regressive, adolescent mood. "No, he seems to like the softer stuff." Our Boyfriends Within can make some surprising mood shifts—even more than most people. But since mine is mostly designed in the nurturing Midge mode, he tends to lean pretty consistently toward the softer side of my CD rack. Less strobe, more candlelight.

Many detailed decisions present themselves when you're beginning to plot dates with your Boyfriend Within. Yet even more important than the details is the single issue brought up by the Voice in his answer: "Get outside yourself." His mystical-sounding advice is indeed key to the entire enterprise. I believe that what my own personal guru is pointing to here is the truth that getting to know a Boyfriend Within is not just a matter of thinking certain thoughts, or feeling certain feelings, or being in a certain mood. There's more involved than our whims, or wishes, or even willpower. The Boyfriend Within is not just an inspirational message. He's not merely bumper-sticker material. He's real.

The saving grace of a "real" friend or significant other, or even an annoying leech of a dubious companion, is that they can take us outside ourselves, occasionally even forcibly drag us outside ourselves. I might be in a funk, but he or she is determined to go to the movies—as I *promised*. Or one evening I'm feeling jet-lagged from a hard day at work and just want to nestle in front of the TV and watch an A&E biography of Jackie O, but a friend has made reservations at a trendy French restaurant with a stiff reservations policy. So I go, unwillingly, only to be introduced to a software company's representative who wants to send me to India to dispatch reports home for their new online travel magazine. The point is that other people can draw us out of ourselves, sometimes with beneficial results.

I assume that my Voice was implying in his answer that a relationship with the Boyfriend Within has some of these same characteristics. That is, he's not just a thought away, summoned up at a moment's notice. You need to approach him more as a commitment requiring some planning, energy, and verve, and less as a lovely pearl for meditation and contemplation. And you need to pursue activities with him in real time and space or, just as with any other relationship, he'll soon become more of a theoretical cipher than an actual option. Prove you care by making room for him in your everyday life.

If you think too much about the Boyfriend Within without taking action or making a date with him, the concept can begin to scatter in a complicated maze of contradictions. Overthinking can lead to paralysis and doubt, to simply getting lost. But the same is true with a Boyfriend Without. If you're serious about someone and are away from that person for a while, you sometimes find disquieting questions presenting themselves, questions that increase in power as they tap into your own paranoia and suspicion: Is this the right person for me? What's wrong with him? Why did he say that? Why is he so distant? Why do I put up with his endless talking about himself? Why doesn't my colleague like him? Does he see something I don't see? Then, with your head still filled with these doubts, the two of you get together for dinner at a new Korean restaurant and—poof!—the questions disappear in the reality of his actual smiling face.

Life with a Boyfriend Within can be filled with distrustful doubts and questions too. The notion that you have a "higher self" or "better half" just waiting to be cultivated and listened to makes sense. That true happiness and satisfaction come from within rather than without has ancient authority. The applicability of these truths to gay men involved in dizzying and sometimes self-destructive or inappropriately adolescent searches for boyfriends as the final solution to a lack of self-esteem is not such a stretch. We can grasp that. But nevertheless the very concept of a Boyfriend Within sometimes becomes a riddle. You can't quite wrap your head around it. And its more comic implications—unseemly narcissism, for instance—take over, undermining whatever benefit could have been salvaged, collapsing the self-help superstructure in an eruption of internal giggles and sneers.

All of these questions and doubts are natural. Have them. I do. But the Voice points to eventually moving beyond such questions. To remain quizzical is to stay paranoid, or paralyzed, or merely cynical. To go beyond the questioning phase requires time and space. It requires actually going on a date with the Boyfriend Within. It requires being in touch with the real thing. So ask the questions, even return to them, but every now and then give yourself a chance to jettison them as well.

In the rest of this chapter I'll be sharing some of my specific experiences and those of my friends in moving past these early doubts and misgivings by actually beginning to date the Boyfriend Within. You might gather some ideas here for your own dates—just as you might clip a recipe for a lamb-and-leek casserole from *The New York Times*. I'm sure, though, that your Boyfriend Within will have his own suggestions, as well as a few of his own ingredients to throw into the pot.

An Evening at Home with the Boyfriend Within

The first official date I went on with my Boyfriend Within was a Sunday evening dinner at home. It had been a long time since I'd cooked for anyone. I'd long ago come to depend on ordering take-out Chinese food, or a cheeseburger and Coke from the diner down the street. When people asked if I cooked, my habitual reply was, "I heat." The only dish I'd prepared for myself in the previous six months was couscous: add boiling water, let sit five minutes. Sometimes the five minutes could be shaved down to three or four: add canned tomatoes, canned tuna fish, then wolf down the concoction in front of the evening news. "Why bother? I'm just eating by myself" was my half-heard inner excuse.

The attraction of such hasty semiconscious dinners was that I didn't have to do much preparatory work. My date with my Boyfriend Within, however, took two hours of preparation. A neighbor advised me to go to a nearby gourmet shop and choose some prepared foods from the counter: a whole chicken, red beets, brown rice, and cranberry juice. Then on to the Korean deli to buy purple-and-gold arrow-shaped flowers (I never did find out their name) and cream-colored candles. Home to vacuum and straighten up; set out a plate, silverware, and a glass; and return phone calls in order to clear the slate of my answering machine.

During dinner I keyed in a selection of Philip Glass minimalist piano music. For a change, I concentrated on what I was eating. (Watching TV with the Boyfriend Within is okay when you're advanced enough, but in early dates it's best to get to know each other in quieter circumstances.) After dinner I loafed on a divan in the living room, listening to the Princess Di funeral CD—especially perking up for John Tavener's haunting, weirdly flat "Alleluia" at the end—while "together" we glanced interestedly through the Sunday *Times*.

The afterglow remained for some time. Somehow all of my couscous dinners in front of CNN—faced too often with the scary pumpkin of Saddam Hussein's face—blended into one fitful dinner. The memory of them is certainly not particularly nourishing and is often tinged with anxiety. The memory of my dinner with the Boyfriend Within, however, has a glow about it. I'm proud of our first evening together. The food we ate somehow turned into a feeling that lasted. Crucial to its power is the message of self-nurturing I was sending to myself, a version of "Whose life is it anyway?" It's a potent benefit delivered much more dependably and lastingly in an action rather than in a mere thought.

The residual effects, too, were quite positive. One of the arguments for funding NASA has been that so many of the discoveries made by indulging in the luxury of space travel are actually applicable on earth— from Tang to thermostats to special cameras to new synthetic fabrics. Likewise my date with the Boyfriend Within turned out to have extra benefits. For the rest of the week I had substantial leftovers in my refrigerator—there had been no such thing as leftover couscous. My floors were dust free. I had candles to light whenever the mood struck.

Taking a Walk with the Boyfriend Within

The poet William Carlos Williams wrote that "most of / the beauties of travel are due to / the strange hours we keep to see them." Well, the beauties of taking a walk with the Boyfriend Within aren't so much due to strange hours. You don't have to get up at dawn; a midnight stroll is a choice, not a requirement. The beauty comes more from a subtle shift of approach.

When I went for my first walk with my Boyfriend Within, I headed to Greenwich Village, a part of town I'd once lived in and thought I knew reasonably well. The entire expedition lasted about an hour and a half. My walk took place on a wintry Saturday as an even light illuminated the neighborhood's nineteenth-century townhouses so they looked as if they belonged in Boston or even Amsterdam. The sky was Parisian—blustery gray blue. I stopped to read all the historical plaques—urban learning aids my Boyfriend Within was drawn to, but which I'd never really noticed before and certainly had never stopped for. I realized that on all my previous walks I'd been on my way somewhere, or had been busily talking with someone. I'd never given myself a chance to see my own neighborhood as might a visitor who'd traveled half a world just to look—dead-on, rather than peripherally.

I made one stop: at a coffee shop. I ordered a Colombian coffee with skim milk. Sat on a stool at a counter to read the complimentary *Times*. That's when I realized that my Boyfriend Within had a strong attraction not only to historical plaques but also to *The New York Times*, much stronger than my own, on my own. I realized then that perhaps a good gift for him for Christmas might be a subscription to the *Times*. (Buying a Christmas gift, birthday gift, even Valentine's gift for the BFW is one of the concepts that will begin to make sense as you advance in your relationship.)

I did feel loneliness sneak up on me every so often, though, as I turned a blank corner, or passed a couple of guys holding hands on a busier thoroughfare. Mostly these sorts of problematic responses are matters for consideration in the next chapter, on "problems with the Boyfriend Within." But I did realize that my fleeting loneliness was: (1) there, and so a feeling to be reckoned with; (2) proof that there is more to life than the Boyfriend Within, as wonderful and overlooked as he may be; and (3) a feeling often plastered over in our rush for the company of others. A walk with the Boyfriend Within—as with any thoughtful companion—can lead as serendipitously to helpful insights, self-knowledge, and so to natural growth, as to a destination successfully hiked to on an arbitrarily chosen map.

Shopping with the Boyfriend Within

Hanging out with the Boyfriend Within can be an opportunity to try new things, sprout new behavior. Like a classic, old-fashioned guy, I've never really liked to shop. Actually I didn't just dislike shopping, I froze or became numb at the concept. I'd be the one left staring into a mound of cotton sweaters—myopic, tense, and lost—while whomever I was with tabulated finds, wished-for gifts, and bargains. A married friend who suffered from the same autistic impulse told me of regularly escaping to smoke five cigarettes while his wife remained inside with a salesman, picking out clothes for him. I had previously either shopped with an expert or relied on hand-me-down's or, when most fortunate, received gifts from designers.

Luckily I live in a popular shopping neighborhood, so I simply turned the corner and started there. First I hit the new Marc Jacobs boutique where I'd seen a black cashmere coat I'd been too neurotic to buy when I'd eyed the thing a few weeks earlier. The store was minimal, stark. And the coat was gone. But as beginner's luck would have it, at the next stop—J. Crew—hung a different black wool-and-cashmere coat. I fingered it, checked out the price tag. (J. Crew was the site of an earlier botched purchase during the summer, when a coat I'd admired wasn't there two weeks later when I finally tapped the strength to return to buy it.)

A seductive salesguy with dreadlocks walked up immediately.

"That's a great coat. We only have four left. You can wear it with anything." His copper eyes were the color of his hair.

So I tried on a medium. "Do you think I need the larger size?" I asked. (A question I'd never been lucid enough to ask before.) He encouraged me toward the large. I stood staring happily into the mirror at a coat that was the male version in black wool of something, cutwise, Jane Jetson might have worn.

"I might as well just go ahead and buy it, then," I said to him, feeling the hard edges of my Amex card in the pocket of my black jeans.

I did receive a rush from that purchase. And was pumped to go on to other stores: Kenneth Cole, Armani, Gap, Banana Republic. I didn't buy anything else, just scanned for information and ideas. But I'd learned some important lessons in shopping—especially the importance of timing, of being prepared for that moment when the intersection of shopper and item add up to an emotional event.

Of course shopping, like the Boyfriend Within, has different meanings for different people. I had a friend whose mother's advice whenever he was feeling unappreciated by the world was, "Go shopping, dear. It'll make you feel better." Since he felt the world owed him a living anyway, her advice only enabled his addiction. His Boyfriend Within might well be asking for a different kind of expedition—like going to Goodwill to donate clothes, perhaps. At least on some of these outings, choose an activity you've historically found challenging—not boring, certainly, but slightly daunting. Your Boyfriend Within may show you a new way through it.

Going to Restaurants, Movies, Museums, Galleries, Ball Games

To go to public events with your Boyfriend Within is yet another step. And one you don't need to force yourself to take. One confidante asked me if I were going to go to a restaurant with my Boyfriend Within. It seemed to be a favorite activity of his. "I'm uncomfortable in restaurants by myself," I answered. "If I'm by myself, I'd rather eat at home." "But you have to," he insisted. "That's the whole point. That you don't care. That you're really not alone; you have the Boyfriend Within."

Well, as my unusually enlightened high school gym teacher used to say when we'd run laps, "You're not trying to set any world records here." Having a Boyfriend Within is not about proving anything to anybody—least of all, yourself. Let the rest of your life be a competition, a trial, an event, a dare if you like—but not this part. Of course if you have the sort of Boyfriend Within who requires adrenaline and new challenges to add briskness to an otherwise dull existence, then by all means go for it. But with Midge as my Inner B, I'm certainly much more prone to let it be. I never force. I do respond, though, to an inner tingle, a half-felt wish. (It's true, too, that many restaurants, including four-star ones, are now featuring "communal tables" or serving dinner for one at areas near the bar where you can eat alone without feeling like a social outcast and perhaps even strike up a casual conversation with a stranger. Or bring along a book you've been meaning to read.)

Going on public dates with my Boyfriend Within is most often about catching up. I have lots of acquaintances, and they expend themselves in lots of different activities. When I'd hear about some of their adventures, I'd wish I'd been there too. But usually, if I couldn't find anyone to go along with me, I would just let the ambition slide: "I have enough work to do at home," I'd tell myself. The Boyfriend Within is the perfect companion to get you out of the apartment and to accompany you on these outings. In one weekend with the BFW, for instance, I caught an Egon Schiele exhibition at the Museum of Modern Art, viewed a documentary about Tibetan medicine, and attended a Golden Gloves boxing match. (My inconsistent Boyfriend Within apparently feels, like Walt Whitman, "I am large, I contain multitudes.")

With your Boyfriend Within it's possible to lead not only a double life, but a fuller life. A great addition to my life, thanks to these dates, is taking in a movie in the middle of the afternoon. Somehow I'd missed this guilty pleasure. Now I indulge regularly. It's a heightened event where the Coke tastes better, and the popcorn too. And it is indeed a case where the "strange hours" kept do add to the beauty of the experience; you can painlessly slip in to see a popular movie that you'd ordinarily need to reserve for by calling 777-FILM for advance tickets, and still you'd wait in line for a half hour to jockey for a decent seat. At noon on Wednesday it's just you, on the aisle, along with a few senior citizens. For this practical luxury, and for the adolescent pleasure of sitting in a darkened movie theater, playing hooky from 9 to 5 adult life, I'm truly grateful. And my squeamishness about tables for one in crowded restaurants definitely doesn't apply to an equally guilty lunch of a Big Mac in the kiddie-colored burger palace a half hour before show time.

"Sure, the lunch counter at Burger Heaven or a

corner table at MacDonald's is safe," a more adventur-
ous friend with a thrill-seeking Inner B protested
when I bragged about my solitary burger. "But what
about a fancier spot?" He put this notion to the test by
going solo to Le Madri, a tie-and-jacket-style northern
Italian restaurant in Chelsea. His lunchtime outing
was a success, and he had a pleasant enough time,
though admitted to removing his glasses to be surrounded by a blur of color and activity without actually feeling the need to participate. "Reality only
intervened when the waiter entered my tiny realm of
vision," he confessed.

Yoga, the Gym, and other Sensual Pleasures with the Boyfriend Within

Talking or even thinking about getting physical with
the Boyfriend Within requires some subtle balancing
and tact. Neuroscientists have been presenting a lot of
evidence lately that the supposed distinction between
mind and body, or thoughts and feelings, is false.
We're really a unified field of energy manifested in different ways, it seems. Yet this philosophical and scien-
tific development doesn't mean that people don't
sometimes *feel* that the body is better left out of discussions of emotional happiness. Blame it on the puri-

tans, I guess. They're always an easy target. But whoever we blame or don't blame, the reality is that getting to know your Boyfriend Within can be as much a physical experience as it is mental, psychological, and emotional.

My favorite physical date with the Boyfriend Within has always been yoga class. My favorite instructor is a young woman with a short pageboy haircut who ends each class with a meditation on following our hearts throughout the week. Her prayerful thought is accompanied by a gesture (or "mudra") of the fingers of our hands pressed together while pointing outward like spokes of a wheel. But the hour and a half before is taken up mostly with stretches, bends, breathing exercises, lunges, squats, twists, turns, and pushes and pulls that uncover creaks and tight spots in my body I never knew were there. Yoga shines an inner light on those hard-to-get-to places. When I leave I feel more flexible, lighter. As the Boyfriend Within is identified with a "higher self," he's also identified with a toned and tuned-up body.

The gym works too. In *What Really Matters: Searching for Wisdom in America,* Tony Schwartz went on a pilgrimage, experimenting with everything from the Human Potential Movement to biofeedback to enneagrams and est. But he wound up being the most straightforwardly positive about weight training as a path to "wisdom," or at least to health and well-being. I've certainly found the aftereffects of working out to be well worth the hour spent, whether due to endorphins, sweat, or the confidence that comes from a cosmetic lift. I usually work with a trainer when weights are involved—I'm still worried they'll crash on my head, or that I'll lunge down and never straighten up again. When I'm working out alone with the Boyfriend Within, however, I tend to aerobics, especially to climbing a stairway to health on the StairMaster, either concentrating on my breathing, or flipping through the week's selection of glossy magazines. One of the mysteries of the gym is the way in which physical exertion can turn thoughts around, reframing a day and opening access to that clearer and more serene atmosphere in which my own BFW thrives.

How the body came to be grounds for deprivation and mortification in popular religions of both the East and West is a matter for scholars of religion. Certainly America has an odd double standard. Sexuality is presented both as the grail of emotional release and fulfillment and as a scarlet, X-rated source of all pain and retribution. The prevalence of sex jokes is just one indicator of the nervous hilarity that surrounds the subject. As I've said, whenever I would talk about the concept for this book, a common reaction was the masturbation joke: "Is it a one-handed manual?"

Whether solo orgasms are part of your relationship with your Boyfriend Within is actually less important than it apparently seems. The outcome falls under the six-of-one, half-dozen-of-the-other category of discernment. What is important is involving your body in your developing awareness of yourself as you expand your relationship with the Boyfriend Within. And not relying invariably on the quick fixes: a video popped into the VCR, an edgy magazine retrieved from under the bed, a stop at the *Playboy* channel. Like quick dinners eaten in front of the TV, or tumbling into an unmade bed surrounded by yesterday's news, the resulting feeling can be as much of stress or distraction as of stimulation and satisfaction. In all these cases, the pleasure of the process is lost in the handy dispensing of the result.

By spending casual time in the bathtub, or on the bed, with the Boyfriend Within, you have the possibility of opening up to a new and richer relationship with your own body. One of the great pluses of getting to know a Boyfriend Within is trying out new behavior, or new approaches to old behavior. Cultivating the garden of your own body, as it were, without the requirements of satisfying someone else or too automatically satisfying yourself, you can begin to explore rhythms and unfettered feelings previously unknown. You can learn the often overlooked thrill and tingle of being in touch with what is no less than Love's body. Few self-gifts are greater, or more steeped in the element of pure pleasure.

As the nature of everyone's Boyfriend Within varies, so naturally do their dates with him. I mentioned in the last chapter that my Boyfriend Within was a Midge type. And so a lot of my dates with him involve relaxing, nurturing activities—dinners at home, yoga, oils and incense. For those whose model is closer to the Jackson Pollock creative Boyfriend Within, their dates might tend more toward getting out canvas and paint, taking a dance class, composing a tune on an electronic keyboard. Or for the thrill-seeking Tony Robbins model, there's always skydiving, mountain climbing, or networking at a local alumni club. One person's date might be another person's job, or snooze.

Don't be afraid to try out a lot of different date concepts. Some will work; some won't. Since my chicken-and-red-beet-dinners from the gourmet shop have become weekly affairs, my diet has been greatly enhanced. As for boxing matches, though, I've left those and other sporting events to group outings. You too will probably find that every date won't be successful for you and your Boyfriend Within. If you find yourself feeling excessively lonely, or bored, that's a bad sign. But gradually you'll find yourself doing a regular "Sunday thing" more often. Or gradually you'll become an expert on movies, or you'll be reading the newspaper every day, or you'll have completed your first one-act play. (Creative dates tend to be among the most popular with many in my immediate circle.)

Just remember to be honest and true to yourself in the dates you choose. This is definitely a case where you'll be getting what you wished for. Like longtime couples, or pet lovers and their dogs, you may find yourself, as time goes on, looking more and more like your Boyfriend Within.

AWARENESS EXERCISE:

7. Plan and go on dates with your Boyfriend Within.

CHAPTER FOUR

QUESTION: *What if I'm having problems with my Boyfriend Within?*

THE VOICE: *You have to meet the Boyfriend Within where he lives, on his own turf.*

EVENTUALLY EVERYBODY SINGS the

blues. There's no getting around it. Indeed, all

those rows of self-help books wouldn't be on

the shelves if readers weren't trying to deal

with, among other things, their own blues: the

kind that seem to sneak up out of nowhere, then sink back again into nothingness, usually unnamed and misunderstood. The great accomplishment of a singer like Billie Holiday was to instill in words and music an emotion that, coupled with the mature beauty of her voice, made a paradox of a great blues song such as "Ain't Nobody's Business If I Do"—a song essentially about a very unbeautiful subject, spousal abuse: "I swear I won't call no copper / If I'm beat up by my poppa." She transmogrifies, even transcends the feeling by dealing with it artistically.

Negative feelings and actions are dross that *can* be turned into gold with a little art or alchemy. In this chapter I'll be talking about those bad feelings, or dubious actions, which can actually be understood as tugs for attention from the Boyfriend Within, as symptoms calling for a cure. It's uncomfortable to have a real-life boyfriend suddenly confronting you angrily at an unexpected moment. But if the confrontation leads to the solution of a conflict you've been ignoring, the momentary unpleasantness is worthwhile in the long run. Some of the sorts of feelings or behavior often indicating you're out of sync with, or, in other words, having problems with your Boyfriend Within are: compulsive behavior, such as lingering for hours in on-line chat rooms, or smoking

a half-pack of cigarettes; feeling exaggeratedly out-
raged at a guy spending too long filling his water bottle in front of you at the fountain at the gym; not
being able to concentrate at work, or in conversations.
The most common and deeply felt siren sounding
from within, though, probably remains those blues
about being lovelorn, or otherwise unhappy in romantic love.

I recently ran into a deejay friend of mine, Rick,
who pedaled up to the curb on his bicycle to tell me
he'd been listening to old tapes from The Saint, the
prime gay New York City disco of the early 1980s. "All
the songs are these masochistic love songs about
wanting love and not getting it and getting dirt kicked
in your face by your beloved," he complained, almost
in a rant, his industrial tattoos peeping from under a
gray muscle shirt. "It was four or five in the morning.
These guys were really vulnerable. They were in a
dance trance under the influence of drugs. And they
were being brainwashed and being told over and over
that love is all about suffering and crying and losing. I
think that's why all these gay men go around behaving like immature high school girls!"

I'm not so sure about the "immature high school
girls" part, but Rick was definitely onto something.
Not that gays have a total monopoly on the attitude

he was describing. The masochistic love song has always been a staple of the music industry. For Diana Ross, love was a hangover for which she didn't want a cure. Prince tabulated the precise count of a lover's departure down to an agonizing "seven hours and fifteen days" in "Nothing Compares 2 U." More than once, Sarah Vaughan made famous songs that were variations on the theme of "The One I Love Belongs to Somebody Else."

I wouldn't want to naïvely point away from the three-way intersection where the often beautiful, sometimes bloody collision can occur between pain, suffering, and beauty. Too much creativity can be traced to that particular accident site. For instance: on the occasion of conducting Handel's *Messiah* for the one-hundred-sixty-ninth time at Carnegie Hall during the Christmas season, David Randolph confessed to *The New York Times* that his relationship with the oratorio had begun at age seventeen, when he was informed by Walta, a girl he loved, that she felt only friendship for him. To ease the embarrassment of the moment, they stepped into a church on lower Fifth Avenue, where a musical performance was in progress. The first sound they heard was a sad melody, a tenor singing the words, "Thy rebuke hath broken his heart." "This was my first exposure to Handel's *Messiah*," he told the *Times*. "I would love to know what has happened to Walta in the intervening six decades and to tell her I perforce thought of her one-hundred-sixty-eight times."

As Randolph's story shows, life has a way of coming up with its own suffering, challenges, disappointments, and rejections. And people occasionally have a way of turning them around. But that doesn't mean there's an imperative to manufacture an extra supply of dross in hopes of accruing an extra supply of gold. The Pollyannaish claim that everything will work out fine if properly approached, or positively thought about, is obviously off. But so is the popular idea that great art can *only* come from suffering or being driven to an early death. The recipe for great love doesn't always have to include obsession, compulsion, and the discomforting feeling of being poised on a cushion of pins and needles.

In this chapter I won't be dealing so much with those essentially tragic situations that are part of the existential infrastructure—war, incurable disease, death: These may or may not be beyond the ken of human wish and choice. Rather, I'll be treating those matters of concern that are still within the purview of our own choice and accountability, things which intimately concern the Boyfriend Within insofar as he's involved with matters of the heart. For it's the heart that sounds the alarm when the Boyfriend Within is troubled. And it's the heart that registers happiness when that positive state occurs. If the Boyfriend Within lives anywhere, he lives in the heart.

Awareness Exercise Eight

List at least five uncomfortable feelings that have made your heart hurt, or made you dizzy enough with fear and anxiety that you couldn't think straight, or have caused you to feel apprehension in your gut. Next to this list of feelings, write down short notes to remind you of actual, remembered situations to which you can connect them. We don't, after all, just have feelings, we have situational feelings.

When checking my own list of crazy patterns in earlier Awareness Exercises against my friends and informants lists, I was always entertained by their variety and dissimilarity. In the lists of troubling emotions, however, I found my own to be almost universally the same as everyone else's. Modulations occur more generally in the spelling out of the situations that create these feelings in different people.

My short list of downers and the situations that helped kick them in included:

- **Hurt**—not invited to a party; overlooked for a promotion at work
- **Angry**—kept waiting an extra fifteen minutes by a workout partner; stood up when someone with whom I had a movie date decided to go dancing instead without bothering to call
- **Jealous**—being the odd man out in a conversation; hearing secondhand about my boyfriend on vacation with an Israeli soldier at the Dead Sea when I thought he was working on a movie in Geneva
- **Lonely**—just walking down the street

The first reaction to doing this exercise is often a heartfelt "Ugh." Some of my casual respondents hadn't been completely comfortable describing their "package" in the earlier Awareness Exercise in chapter 2, but those discomforts were funny, involving a sort of hesitation that seemed humorous. Wading into less pleasant emotions is a bit tougher. But again, it's ground that needs to be cleared. It's a room, as it were, that needs cleaning. Once you have your list and have written down accompanying memories, you'll be able to pick yourself up again. Not that there won't be rough moments in life ever again. But you'll see that a more buoyant and productive condition will be more consistently possible.

In the next exercise we'll be reshooting the primal scenes that we've allowed to bother us and to send us into these downward spins. And by reshooting them, we'll be able to change, thankfully, their emotional tenor and, thus, to expand our emotional options for the future. A wise, tough art history professor once told me—vis-à-vis I forget what—"You choose your feelings." Her comment made no sense to the eighteen-year-old me. By working on the next exercise, however, I began to experience directly what she meant and to put her meaning into action.

Awareness Exercise Nine

Revisit the territory of each of the feelings listed above and each of the situations from which they sprang, then reimagine them. That is, instead of the usual tack of simply reliving, returning again and again to the scene of the crime searching for the culprit responsible for such unfairness, just re-create things differently. It doesn't matter whether you write down your thoughts in full sentences or in short phrases that mean something mostly to you. The point is to try to think how you could have handled those moments differently to create a different emotional result. Use your notes as cues to re-visualize, or as I've said, borrowing a metaphor from the movies, reshoot the scene.

Here are a few of my notes on different situations. You're free, though, in this exercise to have pages and pages of thoughts:

- **Hurt**—not invited to a party

    Reshooting: Maybe the invitation went to the wrong address. Send change-of-address cards.

    or,

    Reshooting: Reviewing the list from the point of view of the hostess, I find that all the guests can help her get ahead in life in ways I can't. She's not thinking *against* me; she's just not thinking of me at all.

- **Angry**—stood up for movie date by someone who didn't call, didn't even apologize

    Reshooting: Expunge him from the credits; recast his part as moviegoing companion with someone more reliable.

- **Jealous**—being the third man out in a conversation

    Reshooting: Imagine what I *might* have said to

interject myself back into the conversation, such as, "Istanbul is my favorite city." Or, "There's going to be more income generated by video games than by movies within five years." Spin words off the top of my head. Next time, talk loosely this way rather than worrying.

- **Lonely**—walking down the street

    Reshooting: Take out my cell phone and line up a date, even if out walking with my BFW when the sensation hits. Make dates until sated and all I want is to be back in Garbo-land.

Experiencing gnawing emotions is certainly not a sign of lack of privilege, standing, or success. It's not the provenance of losers and geeks. In a "Talk of the Town" item in *The New Yorker*, for instance, a well-known art dealer revealed for an entire group of achievers the dynamics of hurt, jealousy, and general paranoia at work in a week of glamorous opening parties for the Getty Museum in L.A. His comments raised the possibility that insecurity actually can be exacerbated by approval and public success. "I have some friends who want to know every person on the guest list so that they can torment themselves as to whether or not they are at the right thing," he said. "I am told it is Richard Meier's night." (The art dealer was himself a guest on that "right" Tuesday night, the night devoted to guests of Meier, the museum's architect.)

I've shared a few of my easier and more straightforward examples. Now, if you're faced with the situation—as I was—of a lover of several years on a secret date in the Middle East, then you might need to think more deeply. Although the lover might be cast as the villain in the scene when it is considered in isolation, the entire movie begins to require a lot of editing to make matters go right. That is, his little fillip of betrayal might actually be traced back to a compressed fist of distance, or resentment, or of lying stretching back into many earlier scenes over many earlier months or years. Extensive reshooting is a tall order, but not an impossibility. Next time, with what you know now, the plot might arc more smoothly in the auteur production of your own life.

I CAST this chapter about these bluesy emotions as "problems with my Boyfriend Within" because such troubling emotions are often signs of being out of touch with the source of happiness and love within. These negative feelings seem to be related to people and events. But they're often actually about an inner relationship that's gotten offtrack. Something's not aligned, and it's usually the mind and the heart. The Voice's prescription is really an indication of the need to become realigned: "You have to meet the Boyfriend Within where he lives, on his own turf." The problems are never with the Boyfriend Within per se. They're always with your relationship to him/her/x/y/z.

These warning signs can also be detected in actions. We all have ways of acting out that help us avoid the tough work of feeling negative emotions and trying to turn them around. E-mailing me on this topic of avoiding negative emotions through obsessive-compulsive behavior, one friend confided, "My first reaction is that for most guys out there the first thing we encounter are obsessive behaviors which preoccupy and keep us away from feeling emotions at all. Some good warning signs I've encountered over the years in that category would be obsessive partying; disco every weekend; obsessing about problems with lovers; obsessive cruising in bars, baths, anywhere the inexhaustible prospect of connection exists; habitual substance use; duh, obsessive buying; obsessive—oh I don't know—list making. . . . I guess the list goes on."

If you've been reading and working your way through this book, you've learned some reliable measures for dealing with emotional or mental crises. Some may have been presented as techniques already;

some, implied. Others may be your own home reme-
dies, concocted during a lifetime of trying to keep
your head above water, or in the process of reading
about and getting to know better the source of rejuve-
nation and general therapeutic uplift you carry
around like a spiritual battery pack within.

Awareness Exercise Ten

Write down the ways you've found to be most effective and most trustworthy for reestablishing your relationship with the Boyfriend Within during difficult
times. That is, when your psychic alarm goes off,
when calls for attention from the Inner B are manifested as dark clouds of gloom or panic or loneliness or
low self-esteem, what best can you do? The four sorts
of activities I've found to be the most helpful in
reestablishing my relationship with the Boyfriend
Within, in giving him the attention he needs to sail
on, are:

- Active, creative expression
- Passive inspiration
- Conversations with the Voice
- Meditation

One sort of active, creative expression that works for me is writing poems. Coinciding often with the first crush of romantic love and the tingling, preliminary apprehension of death in adolescence, poetry can be a way of letting the drops of blood splatter where they may. For adults who don't go on to become masters of the craft, this art sometimes diminishes over time as the weapon of choice for bloodletting. But I still hold onto poetry as a choice response for a system in chaos, unable to focus, just needing to get "it" out. (Poetry, of course, has plenty of other more high-minded uses in the culture, including crossing beyond the set borders of language and thought.) Less formally freighted and often equally effective is just taking pen to paper and writing down on a pad, or in a journal, the swirl of distraught words until a calm clarity returns.

Creative expression doesn't need to be confined to writing. Other choices can be visual, visceral, or musical. You could try finger painting, for example. There's something about the sheer childishness of this activity that makes me feel I'm totally involved in getting at angst rather than trying to impress someone or make something that will be suitable for framing. (It's important to find ways to sidestep any feelings of performance or audience. You should be doing this for yourself.) Making collages—especially those incorporating photographs from childhood—can give shape and jagged significance to an unconscious jumble. Composing aleatory music on piano or drums or guitar helps. Even banging a tennis racket on a bed, or thumping a pillow, can be percussive, tribal, purgative. The important point is just to keep at it—painting or writing or thumping—until the mood has lifted.

A second useful activity for getting back in touch with the Boyfriend Within is that of more passive inspiration, by which I mean going for a little more of what the poet Keats called "wise passivity." That is, kick back and soak in whatever you've found to be helpful, consoling, or inspiring to you. Reading is certainly an example, although not just reading for reading's sake, or not even reading for pure entertainment's sake—as *relaxing* as a spin with Ann Rice's vampires or John Grisham's lawyers might be. I'm thinking more of those few books on the shelf that reliably have acted as a match to the sentimental pilot light of your heart. A few of my old faithfuls are: Rainer Maria Rilke's *Letters to a Young Poet;* Thomas Merton's *Seeds of Contemplation;* or, occasionally, even Marianne Williamson's *A Return to Love.*

Music is also famously a hot bath, a "charm / To make bad good," as Shakespeare wrote. Again, the music you choose might not be what you'd put on when a guest comes over. It might not even be what you critically consider to be the best music. Certainly the books I listed above aren't on my list of the great works of literature—but then *The Brothers Karamazov* is not a book I'd reach for in a crisis. I admire Richard Strauss's difficult musical composition *Metamorphosen* as much as the next "dead white European male," but in a crunch I tend more toward the religious or melodic: *Chant,* by the Benedictine monks of Santo Domingo de Silos, or Samuel Barber's mournful *Adagio for Strings.* Don't be afraid to short-circuit your critical capacities in an emergency. It's one of those lifesaving secrets that can be kept squarely between you and your best interests. You won't be graded on it.

I've certainly discussed the Voice quite a bit in these pages. Yet I feel that the Voice can never be overestimated. The ultimate payback is the day when you find yourself free enough of angst and distraction to take time to ask the Voice some of the big questions, such as those heading each chapter in this book. These are highlighted moments when you really begin to think for yourself. In this developing—in private— of opinions on ultimate values and direction, you're actually developing a philosophical home base, a world of experience and meaning to share with your

Boyfriend Within. It might sound crazy, but it's truly (I think) as sane as it gets.

Meditation, too, can soothe a savage breast. What I now think of as meditation has developed in my own life from childhood prayers and from time spent in a contemplative Trappist monastery, and extends through to Eastern meditative techniques learned from books, seminars, and yoga classes. The sort of meditation you need for getting in touch with the BFW has little to do with magical acts of transcendence. You don't need to stand on your head atop a cold mountain. Certainly for advanced practice you would want to become part of a group, or hook up with a teacher with whom you feel comfortable, but for getting back in touch with the Boyfriend Within, the basics work fine.

Meditation as I'm envisioning the activity for the purpose at hand is just sitting quietly with the Boyfriend Within. It's spending time together. I try to do this for a half hour each day. First I read a bit. I run through a sort of checklist of conscience, of wishes and goals. It's my warm-up. This is also a good time for a back-and-forth with the Voice. Then I settle into simply breathing, following the rhythm of inhalation and exhalation, trying to let go of all the thoughts of the day. If distractions come up, and I find that I'm off and running after them, I breathe more deeply, erase the chalkboard as it were, and patiently begin over again. Breathing in. Breathing out. Often an involuntary smile will come over my face. That's a sign of progress—a sort of "hello" from the Boyfriend Within. Rather than finding the solution to a particular problem, the idea is that you have a feeling of relationship with your own source of power and contentment within, which is a general solution to almost all of the problems presenting themselves each day.

Some people establish a routine of meditating at a certain time every day, in a certain room, on a certain pillow. The repetition helps them return more easily, by power of suggestion and habit, to the state of mind associated with that time and place. I tend to meditate in the same room, on the same pillow, but at different times, according to convenience. Certainly if I'm feeling out of alignment with my Boyfriend Within, I use meditation as an emergency measure to get back in touch, whenever and wherever I am. If practiced regularly, meditation can become an agreed-upon meeting place between you and your Boyfriend Within. Of course, so can all of the practices I've listed, as well as other practices you may have invented and listed for yourself. For one friend, swimming is always the answer. Trust the ones that work for you.

•   •   •

My favorite contribution from street slang in the past year or so has been the phrase "Peace out!"—a perfect cap for describing the aftereffects of meditation in a world of action. It's an amalgam of the old hippie wish, "peace," with the "over/out" of, say, a jet fighter pilot. This mixed message allows the feeling of an open-ended blessing to come through benevolently, while maintaining some of the hard edge appropriate for a world in which war and peace, technology and spirituality must coexist.

If nothing else, the Rx of this chapter has called for peace-ing out, for withdrawing from an unequal struggle with self-created pain. By turning within, you'll be able to show up more naturally and effectively the next time you need to—for a person, or an event. *Out* is the natural direction for an overflow of peace that can come after time spent with the BFW, working through bad feelings or insecurity.

To quote the last line of a poem by the artist and poet Joe Brainard:

"PEOPLE OF THE WORLD: RELAX!"

AWARENESS EXERCISES:

8. List five uncomfortable, negative emotions. Next to the list, write down short notes about actual, remembered situations to which you can connect them.

9. Review the list of situations in Awareness Exercise Eight and write down notes for reshooting them to change their outcome.

10. List techniques for reestablishing your relationship with the Boyfriend Within that you've found to be most reliable in difficult times.

CHAPTER FIVE

QUESTION: *How does the Boyfriend Within relate to a Boyfriend Without?*

THE VOICE: *The Boyfriend Within will enhance your connection with your Boyfriend Without, not to mention with your Boyfriend(s) Without, your friendships and your partnerships.*

ABOUT TWO DAYS after the Voice gave his answer to my question for this chapter, a photographer friend coincidentally announced to me on the phone: "This next year's going to be all about friendships and partnerships. That's where the lasting commitments come from. Those other kinds of relationships don't last. The needy, fake ones. The ones based on sex." I'm not denying there was a bitter tinge to his pronouncement, but there's no denying its essential wisdom either.

While mulling over this topic of the relevance of the Boyfriend Within to all the rest of our relationships, especially primary ones, I was serendipitously given a few more insights in conversations during the following weeks. It seemed appropriate that help in thinking about this subject come from voices outside—much like the photographer's sudden and unsolicited comment.

A second insight came from a psychotherapist who told me she'd conducted a group therapy session in New Jersey. A woman shared with the circle that after being divorced, she needed to find a new husband to help complete her new life. She went into cognitive therapy, attended singles' events, and ordered a sizable pile of books and videotapes on dating, courtship, and second marriages. One day, though, she woke up realizing that this second phase of her adult life was just fine without a new husband. Since that revelation she's actually remarried, but in the interim between the time of her realization and the event of actually meeting the right mate, she'd been content, relaxed, even flourishing. The change had certainly made her life easier. Perhaps by giving up on the aggressive, binocular-focusing search mode she had adopted, she paradoxically made the meeting of her second husband possible.

A third contribution came from a friend at a Sunday brunch. We began talking almost like anthropologists about the mating practices of gay men. Pretty soon the words and observations were tumbling so quickly, and overlapping so chaotically, that it's impossible for me to remember who said what when.

"What if we stopped going to bars and clubs and started looking to our friends for partners instead?"

"That happens sometimes. Guys have been friends for five years and then all of a sudden turn to one another and realize they've fallen in love without even trying."

"Is that crazy?"

"It's the reverse of the usual. Among gay men, sex is like a handshake, a way of saying hello. Then the sex often disappears gradually."

"Not always."

"Right, right. . . . But this way it would sort of grow from a glimmer to a gleam over months or years. It's a wild thought."

"Commitment might be more lasting that way. At least you'd know what you were getting."

"Less like Lotto?"

The gist here was that gay men often search outside their circle of friends for some equivalent of a tall, dark stranger. It's almost like a hunter going into the woods in search of his prey. Rather than kill it, however, the gay man drags back his exotic find, with whom he's become romantically involved. Often this tall, dark stranger eventually becomes domesticated and fits within the known circle of friends, thus changing his status from prey to fellow hunter, and the cycle begins again. (Of course such maneuvers occur in straight society as well, though more often marriage partners seem to be drawn from among friends of friends, or fellow guests met at a dinner party. Perhaps the particularly feisty man-man combination of gay male life—as opposed to man-woman—is responsible: Lesbians also seem to operate more often *within* an established social circle.)

Those three conversations all helped me to begin to clear up for myself the Voice's initially enigmatic-sounding answer to this question of what the Boyfriend Within could possibly mean to someone who's dating, or involved in a relationship: "The Boyfriend Within will enhance your connection with your Boyfriend Without, not to mention with your Boyfriend (s) Without, your friendships and your partnerships."

The basic concept behind the Boyfriend Within is simple, universal, and commonsensical—happiness comes largely from within. Certainly this is true to a greater extent than our culture generally appears to accept. Because of the commonsense aspect of this belief, we perhaps have a tendency to take its implications too lightly, to think it simply can be assimilated and then worn casually. But actually there is a domino effect that comes into play here, and it can have a substantial impact. Once we begin changing our attitude toward ourselves, we necessarily begin changing our attitudes toward others and toward the meaning of our friendships and love affairs and long-standing commitments. That is, if you go there, you'll begin in the ensuing months to reevaluate much more than your personal moods and habits—the effects can be far reaching and complex.

The Boyfriend Within turned out for me to be a sort of Archimedes' lever. The world that could be measured by the concept expanded gradually from a personal to an interpersonal one. The need for change had been signaled in the beginning in a negative way: I felt I couldn't connect; my circuitry was fouled up. Now the change was beginning to be signaled in a positive way. I began to feel . . . well . . . friendlier. The repercussions of that friendliness are the stuff of this chapter.

If you believe that your own happiness is dependent on someone else, you are going to give that person a lot of control over you—power to make you happy, power to frustrate you, and power to destroy you emotionally. A prospective mate can suddenly have license to behave in ways unacceptable for anyone else in your life. But if you keep the stress on the second syllable—emphasizing the "friend" in "boyfriend"—you can begin to lighten up and have your wits about you as well. This doesn't mean that romance won't ever strike. But you will come to appreciate a new acquaintance for exactly who he is, not for how close he comes to delivering word-for-word the script you've assigned him in the play of your life—a play which, if staged on that principle, would be a revival at best. Rose-colored glasses don't always make things look better after all, just more baroque.

By our starting off on a friendlier footing, the basis on which we carry on a relationship can then shift. It's like the adjustment described in the old wives' saying about marriage: "The first time is for love, the second time for money." What's meant by "love" in this context is probably fireworks at midnight, over Central Park on New Year's Eve, viewed from the perfectly located crystal bay window. That is, romance. But what's meant by "money" can perhaps be broadened to include a few things other than cash in the bank—job, achievement, access to a compatible social world. It might sound harsh and unvalentinelike of the Voice to appear to be bringing deal making and business into the discussion, but then love and friendship, if they're real, are grounded in body as well as soul, bank as well as bed, persona as well as person.

Addressing the question of relationships is at least as complex as addressing everyone's Inner B, because different readers are involved in different sorts of relationships, or are situated at different points on the life curve. Basically, though, there are three choices, each of which *I've* certainly opted for in some form at one time or another: married; single; dating. The relationship of the Boyfriend Within to the first two is relatively straightforward. As dating is a more fluid experience, the relationship between the inner and the outer boyfriend in this third case becomes more fluid, complex, and strategic. If you're involved in one situation, you're certainly free to skip the Awareness Exercises targeted for a different situation. But then curiosity about what your peers are up to might draw you in. For most of us, all three cards tend to be played eventually.

"Married"

"Marriage" for gay people is still an open-ended institution. It remains, as Melville said of life, "a voyage out," rather than a trip with a defined itinerary. Statistics indicate that in our society, the institution of marriage continues, but under the sign of the question mark. High divorce rates indicate ambivalence and confusion. Yet, just when straight couples are chafing under the restraints of marriage agreements, many gay political leaders are struggling to make the institution available to all. Jurisprudence in Hawaii appears ready to allow gay marriages. The State of New Jersey is now permitting two men to jointly adopt a child—a sideways form of tentative, indirect approval.

Across the nation, a few gay men have been married in a civil, lay, or religious ceremony; more have exchanged "friendship rings." For most, however, "marriage" is self-defined: You're married if you say you're married. For purposes of this book, when I'm discussing marriage, I'm speaking of being in a primary relationship with one person in which there's some mutual understanding of commitment coupled with a long-term view, even if there's an awareness of the flexibility and fragility of such vows and views;

that is, of the quixotic nature of the noble enterprise. Certainly my eleven-year relationship, including seven years of living together, was in many ways like a marriage.

I went to a traditional wedding ceremony once where the officiating priest, in his short homily to the bride and groom, interpreted the line, "I take this man to be my lawful wedded husband. . . ." He said that what it largely meant was that "I *don't* take Jack, or Fred, or Barney. . . ." That is, the commitment to one person is implicitly a giving up of lots of other people, at least as a wife or husband. (Episcopalians have never been much for harems or polygamy.) One of the signs of being in a more "married" state is that others have been excluded from that particular niche of heart and life. The deal in terms of how involved you may become with those others—Jack, or Fred, or Barney—is then worked out case-by-case by each couple, either together or unilaterally, in negotiation or on the sly.

"Letting go" forms a significant undertow to being married, or even to just the feeling of being married. "It's like letting go of the handlebars," someone once remarked to me of the trust and commitment involved. By stepping onto the same vessel and floating away from shore, a couple's opportunity for a mutually focused adventure is made more possible. Somehow the wind in the sails is this very commitment to one course and the abandonment of shorter, more varied day trips. Yet once underway and "out at sea" so to speak, rough moments arise. Even in the closest of marriages, solitude and aloneness recur. It's at these moments that the Boyfriend Within can make his helpful presence known, becoming a stand-in, surrogate, companion, or guide.

Awareness Exercise Eleven

List a few occasions in your life with a Significant Other when you suddenly felt thrown back on your own resources, or left alone. Then using the skills you used in the Awareness Exercises in the last chapter, make notes for reshooting the scene: Write down how you might have handled the situation differently—or even just thought about the situation differently—if you'd been as tuned in to the Boyfriend Within as you're hopefully becoming by now. (Remember that such reshooting isn't just wishful thinking, fantasy, or imagination. It may directly change the way these scenes will play themselves out in the future at unexpected junctures.)

I found that my list, and those of a few of my

friends, usually contained three types of potential wake-up calls. The first tend to be work-related separations, and these are the easiest for the Boyfriend Within to help salvage:

- I was "married" to a filmmaker who was forever going away on shoots that could last for weeks, or even months, here and abroad.
- I was later involved with an actor who would enter into speeded-up, intense periods of work.
- A friend's boyfriend, an architect, recently went to work in Toronto for three months.
- Another's boyfriend of several decades has moved to the Carolinas simply because he could not function anymore in the city: They spend a weekend a month, and large chunks of vacation time together.

The reshooting of these moments usually involves some version of the dating of the Boyfriend Within concept from chapter 3. The reaction of the partner "left behind" in these situations can be that he's left holding the bag, or keeping the home fires burning. Such curatorial work is ego challenging. Suddenly you feel you're a minor employee rather than a full partner in the firm. Many of the kinder, gentler customs of being together—simply keeping the place tidy, making sit-down meals, taking a movie break—are found to have been based on being a couple. A more positive revision of these feelings can come about by using this time for intensive sessions with the Boyfriend Within (checking in with the Voice every hour?) and for learning to make life comfortable and cushioned not just for an *us,* but for you (videos for one?).

In one of my own examples for Exercise Eleven, for instance, my solution for reshooting was clearly evident to me in retrospect:

* My filmmaker boyfriend was away for five months, working in Europe.

   Reshooting: Instead of cursing him under my breath, or feeling mopey and lonely, I use the opportunity to redecorate; to take lessons in northern Italian cooking and put them to good use; to have a party.

More challenging are those situations of the second type, in which you feel you're being insensitively upstaged, or you're dealing with problems of your partner's that only become yours by proxy. I've been disturbed when:

- A lover came home hours late
- He didn't come home at all
- He went off for an extended weekend in the country with someone else

First off, these more serious ruptures require talking things out with your partner, and perhaps even counseling. You have to know what you've agreed to in the first place. If vows are being flippantly broken, then it's definitely time to talk. If differences are irreconcilable, you can always choose to move on. For example:

- He didn't come home at all.

  Reshooting: Instead of turning my face to the wall for a few days, we talk when it first happens; if there's a second time, we check into couples' counseling.

Either way, you can use these upsets as additional opportunities to take care of yourself. Often the feeling that "He doesn't love me"—whether justified by events or not—is a warning-in-disguise from within that you're not loving *yourself* enough. Much anger and frustration can be dissipated by simply dropping everything for a good, long session of loving self-indulgence. After this soul sifting, take care of whatever problems remain.

The third sort of problems are profound dilemmas that can take away the body, or spirit, of a partner. Examples are:

- AIDS
- Drug dependency
- Depression

These more extraordinary situations require the taking on of an additional role with your partner so you're able to be an effective nurse, tough-love coach, or angel. The Boyfriend Within now becomes more of a special energy source that can be tapped for its supply of heat, energy, love, and compassion. The more serious the problem, the more profound and mystical the qualities required of, and usually provided by, the BFW. Cultivate him now if you want to be assured of being delivered during such crises later.

- Drug dependency
  Reshooting: Instead of thankfully watching him shuffle off to scream therapy, I become involved in his therapy and start a focused program of my own to examine why I allowed

myself to pretend I didn't know about the problem, or felt unable to help him overcome it.

Finally, in marriage you must respect your partner's Boyfriend Within as scrupulously as you do your own. Otherwise there'll be trouble. I had a partner who decided to fly by himself to a resort of chic shacks on the beach in Jamaica for New Year's. I couldn't believe he didn't want to take me. Was he really going to read those four bestselling novels he packed? My mind played tricks about who he was meeting, and why. I found it much harder to sincerely believe that *his* Boyfriend Within was asking for time and space—with no particular reflection on me—than to listen to the sometimes irrational wishes of *my* BFW. It turned out that he really was simply off on his own no-pressure holiday.

Single

In a sense this entire book has been a meditation on the nature of being single, since we're all somewhat single even if married or dating. It's been an updating and hopefully a deepening of one of the first successful self-help books, Helen Gurley Brown's *Sex and the Single Girl,* from the sixties. Of course "Sex" by now has evolved to "Sex, Romance, Love, and Spirituality," and "The Single Girl" to "The Singular Guy/Girl." And just my comfort at being able to telegraph to you such a boggling notion at this point means that this section can be short, a tying up of a few loose ends. That is, you already know it all.

Awareness Exercise Twelve

Write a paragraph in which you express why you've chosen to be—or by accident or design have found yourself—single at this moment in your life. If you're not single, write a paragraph in which you express why you've chosen not to be.

Here are my thoughts on the subject:

- By looking within rather than without for happiness, love, and support, I've coincidentally drained a lot of the air out of my tires as far as the old motivations go for looking for a boyfriend, lover, partner, mate. I now enjoy all my partnerships and friendships in all their subtle colorings and shadings. If one of these relationships should grow into something more primary, or more romantic, I'd obviously be happy and pleasantly surprised. More power to us. But I'm not beginning with the end in mind.

Your thoughts on being single, your point of view on this existential condition, will be especially crucial in determining the quality of your life should you decide to move on to the next phase, dating.

Dating

To date well, to discover the Zen of dating, you need to be flexible. You need to be having fun. I didn't always feel that way before I meditated and acted on the notion of the Boyfriend Within—until its repercussions became part of my own experience. In fact I often said "I don't date." And I often didn't. Partly the notion seemed corny and better left to teenagers—a time in my life when my dates with girls were disasters of shyness, subterfuge, embarrassment, and ineptitude. But mostly, in my adult life, I'd decided that dates were the equivalent of job interviews. That both partners were really interviewing each other for a certain job with a certain job description. The slacker in me just couldn't participate. I balked.

Awareness Exercise Thirteen

Whether married, single, or dating, make a short list of four or five people you'd *like* to date. They can be famous. They can be crushes. They can be sexual or nonsexual attractions. They can be people already in your life who you simply enjoy being with for no particular reason. Indeed, "for no particular reason" is important here. This one exercise is simply about having fun, taking a break. Just because you're already going out with someone doesn't mean you want him on this list. You should make this a completely irresponsible wish list, not a test to see how you view yourself, and certainly not a list of people with whom you'd necessarily want to make a life commitment. It's a list that probably would be completely different five days from now, five months from now, even five minutes from now. For comic relief, you can even add a movie star. Consider it more as a mood ring than a wedding band. At best, it will help take the edge off an activity that has perhaps become *overly* weighted with import.

My list, off the top of my head, a Polaroid of a moment of wishful mental time, is:

- Brian
- Keanu Reeves
- Bret
- Tough Thug (on-line screen name)

Feel free to mix gay and straight, men and women, people you really know and movie stars. Or not.Be as conservative or as radical as you want at the moment.

THE revelation in my own life has been the discovery that the source of security and pleasure many of us have been searching for is probably at the center of our lives rather than spinning on the periphery. This revelation had its most palpable aftershocks in my dating life, and more profoundly in my entire view of relationships with guys, girls, friends, boyfriends, lovers, and even business partners. I'm sure the Boyfriend Within is universal, no matter what name he goes under. I'm not so sure that the implications I've found concerning the Boyfriend Without will *necessarily* be your implications. That's between you and your Voice. But I suspect they might be.

What happens when you stop expecting to find

the qualities of your Boyfriend Within in a Boyfriend Without? And what are the implications for dating? And for your life? A first response might be, to reiterate the words of a bluesy number, "Is that all there is?" Or the ambiguously slanted title of a recent movie about romantic oscillation, *As Good As It Gets*—meaning that when you finally land on your feet, there's a sinking feeling of nowhere left to go. You're a disappointed Alexander the Great with no more lands to conquer. Hunting season has been declared over. So what to do now on weekends?

Awareness Exercise Fourteen

List real or possible reactions to the condition of no longer looking at the world as a mail-order catalog from which you're hoping to pick out the best possible boyfriend. If you stop shopping, you might feel let down at first. But other interesting feelings might soon begin to well up to fill the void. For some, including me, the world begins to open out more and more into that sixties paradigm: "a better place."

Among the discoveries I've made, and you might make:

- Suddenly looking romantically at a friend of ten years
- Hanging out almost exclusively with people who make me feel good, who excite me, or who seem emotionally open and available; not doing the reverse—hanging onto a chore of a person for the sake of a "relationship"
- Sleeping with friends; or conversely, spending more time with someone to whom I'm romantically attracted, but, for one reason or another, I won't be sleeping with anytime soon, if ever

I'm emphasizing the "fun" involved here because many interested parties have expressed fears about going too far with the Boyfriend Within. "It sounds like you're giving up sex and romance," someone complained. "Who wants that?" Actually, though, sex and romance remain very much present, perhaps even more pervasively present when you begin to dance with partners while keeping centered on the Boyfriend Within. Rather than being easily labeled, sex and romance become a more volatile, mysterious part of everyday encounters. In essence, you bring all the adrenaline and excitement of the hunt in the dark woods into the circle of your daily life. Everyone's circle can become charmed. It's a kind of white magic.

I'm not denying the difficulties here. Living against the grain takes some spunk and even more resilience. You're not always going to be up to the task. Sometimes you're going to forget about your BFW, or not be able to conjure him up, or even feel abandoned by him. That's when you might find yourself on some deserted street, stalking your fantasy at midnight during a full moon, and wonder how you got there. Or you'll be acting out your anxiety about a blank Friday night with nothing to do by playing too many video games, or smoking too many cigarettes, or drinking too many beers. If you begin to navigate by your Boyfriend Within, though, this too shall pass. You'll gradually come to be more and more under his influence, and your life will change by gradations. Just go easy on yourself during the inevitable periods of backsliding and regression. You'll soon be back on course.

The opposite concern is that this is all too easy, a mere concession to the Peter Pan complex of not wanting to grow up. It's true that allegiance to your Boyfriend Within can spare you many entangling adult responsibilities, but it will be only those that are self-defeating and slightly dishonest. Being freed in this manner is finally not a self-serving, rootless way to live. Indeed it's only when freed from needy, false love—from looking for love in all the wrong places—that a truly mature love can begin to grow.

Without the obvious calls to responsibility and other-directed behavior provided by a traditional wife or husband, children, or extended family, gay people sometimes appear to be living in a vacuum, in a self-referential spinning top of a "me" world. As I discuss in the next chapter, however, the Boyfriend Within eventually turns out—surprisingly, given the narcissistic-seeming tinge to the concept—to provide oxygen that can transform that very vacuum into commitment, contribution, and selfless service.

Awareness Exercises:

11. List a few occasions in your life with a Significant Other when you suddenly felt thrown back on your own resources, or left alone. Then write down notes about how you might reshoot the scene—how you might have handled, or even thought about, the situation differently.

12. Write a short paragraph in which you express why you've chosen to be—or by accident have found yourself at this moment—single. If you're not single, write a paragraph in which you express why you've chosen not to be.

13. Compose a wish list of at least four people with whom you'd like to go on a date.

14. List real or possible reactions to no longer looking at the world as a mail-order catalog from which you're trying to pick out the best possible boyfriend.

CHAPTER SIX

QUESTION: *What's love got to do with it?*

THE VOICE: *Love is the selfless work you do for another. Love makes you feel loved.*

ONE EVENING I was having supper at a macrobiotic restaurant with a playwright friend who was explaining to me more plaintively and stridently than usual why he particularly needed a boyfriend in order to lead a fulfilled life. I decided not to just nod sympathetically, but to get down in the trenches with him and try to work this through.

"What is it that you expect to get out of this relationship that's so different from what you get from your friendships?" I asked sincerely.

"I want to feel love," he said. "I want to love and be loved. It's not the same as friends."

"Well, if you want to have that feeling of love in your heart, why not volunteer to work in a soup kitchen or something?" I suggested.

My easygoing friend looked positively angry. His face burned reddish. One eyebrow peaked upward. I realized that I'd said the wrong thing, that I'd definitely pushed some button.

"I give back to the world through my writing," he shot back. "That's my contribution. I'm not talking about *that* kind of love."

I promptly dropped the subject. Now I probably would never have made such a lofty-sounding remark if I hadn't recently had an experience with the very phenomenon I was trying to discuss. What sounded like a non sequitur to my friend actually possessed a logic for me.

The inspiration I was drawing on for my unwelcome suggestion during our dinner of scrambled tofu and steamed vegetables had occurred during my then-recent New Year's retreat at the ashram in the Catskills. That's when I'd had my first experience with selfless service, or *seva* as it is called. During my five-day stay, our daily activities were supposed to include stopping by a central office to be assigned a few hours of unpaid duty for the community at large, such things as dishing out oatmeal in the cafeteria, serving as an usher in the main meditation hall. As a mark of service completed, you received a star pasted on your identification badge. This notion of *seva* rankled me at first, so much so that I resolved to steer clear. I wasn't going to be ripped off by having to perform mindless work for zero pay.

Curiosity, guilt, and boredom finally got to me, however. So on the last possible day I filled out a form with my qualifications. With no discernible reference to all those skills I'd snappily listed, I was assigned work on an upcoming musical pageant about a thirteenth-century Hindu saint. My job was to tape pieces of black felt over chinks in the screens at the back of the stage. I learned how to cut swatches with a razor, thanks to an entertainment lawyer from L.A., and met a half dozen new people on the crew. That night at the production I couldn't help admiring the sheer blackness of the backdrops and side drops. I felt strangely proud. And the community effort involved—the novelty of moving forward a project that wasn't my own—did leave a sweet, burning sensation in my heart.

I thought back to that uplifting session of cutting and taping while talking to the frustrated playwright, and to that time when I wrote down the Voice's answer to my question about love and the Boyfriend Within—"What's love got to do with it?" Click! I suddenly understood the leap involved in going from the question—which I'd been thinking of purely in terms of *romantic* love—to the answer. But it's a leap everyone can't necessarily follow at first.

"I need somebody to love," another friend said to me, echoing both the playwright *and* the Beatles. "I want somebody to love." If someone says this to you, and your first reaction is, "Well, go work in a soup kitchen," I can promise that you're not going to get very far. But the more you begin to think about the issue—with the help of a Boyfriend Within, strengthened by lots of attention over weeks and months—the more you might begin to arrive at an explanation, a justification that makes sense to you. But *only* if you've been regularly practicing love and care for the subtle needs of your Boyfriend Within all along. Just as you have to be twenty-nine before you're thirty, I don't think you can understand or create much love before you're thoroughly happy.

The oddity of my spiritual work-study program at the ashram had been the linking together of a feeling with a contradictory stimulus. The feeling was a glowing in the heart—which, of course, is the phenomenon of love. Such love is a one-size-fits-all response: It's the same whether evoked by a kiss, or the giving or receiving of a gift, or the adoption of a child, or a warm hug on a crowded street. It's the reward of caring. Boyfriends and lovers present each other lots of opportunities for creating this feeling: bringing home flowers, remembering a birthday, calling up and apologizing after a misunderstanding. But mundane life presents lots of opportunities too. Even dumb manual labor can be one of them, if the meaning is there.

If you're like the playwright, you've probably resisted the Voice's conclusion. Counting up cards received on Valentine's Day seems more appealing. Yet the more you think about it, the more convinced you may become that the Voice is onto something. Or more accurately, the more you *feel* your way into the subject, the more convinced you may become. This chapter is really about learning to be "warmhearted," which means learning to warm up your own heart and, by extension, those of others. To love and be loved by the Boyfriend Within is to feel that warmth—and to try to sustain its glow as long as possible.

Luckily you won't need to travel to an exotic, multicultural ashram in the Borscht Belt to activate this love within—to set up a call-and-response dynamic of love between you and your Boyfriend Within. You can start where you live. And you don't even need to start with a burning cause, or even a charitable organization, church, mosque, or synagogue. The first circle you can begin to heat up is the immediate one that includes your friends, family, colleagues, and acquaintances. This is your circle of influence. It's been tailor-made by you, for you. And those who loom largest within its circumference are the perfect subjects with whom you can begin to practice love.

"What's this?" I asked a freelance editor recently as I sauntered over to his workstation in a corner of his apartment. Stuck on the wall was a yellow Post-it with the message, "Make one nonbusiness call today!" "Oh, that's just a reminder; if I don't see it, I don't do it," he responded when I asked its significance. The reminder, he went on to explain, was designed to make him reserve one phone call a day—out of the scores he makes as a freelance editor—to someone who was not a client, a business prospect, or a potential sex partner. He told me how rare such calls had become in his life. And how satisfying the results of the calls when he made them. No matter how the recipient responded on the other end, he knew he was fueling his own fire. This was a kind of warmth he'd been missing before he began obeying his Post-it. Such "selfless" calling didn't come naturally at first. The force of resistance can be surprising. And yet the heart is structured as a matching fund. Give it an excuse, and you'll be feeling that initial warmth spontaneously several times afterward. That is, put one log on the fire, and you've got the equivalent of a Duraflame throughout the day.

What you're likely to find is that "selfless" action is really not selfless at all. It's self-ish, even, depending on your definition. I had a movie-actor friend who was in an car accident in L.A. He moved back to New York City for therapy and rehabilitation. Large chunks of his memory had been erased, at least temporarily. It seemed that getting together with him would be a chore. Some of his friends avoided him entirely. Taking my editor friend's Post-it suggestion, I put my actor friend's name on my list of charitable calls. Not only did I feel good for doing something without an immediate personal payoff, I discovered that our friendship—on the phone, in person—was as deeply rewarding as before in fun, communication, and even in fueling the slight crush I'd always had on him. I was getting double bang for my buck.

Well-meaning activity is in that special class of work that doesn't necessarily present its rewards up front. Physical exercise would be another. When my alarm clock goes off at 7:30 in the morning to rouse me to see my trainer, all I want to do is to press the snooze button. And yet by the time I've left the gym, I'm invariably energized. It's a gift I give to myself that keeps being rewarding throughout the day, and often over the next day or two. Yet if I followed my initial feeling about the enterprise, I wouldn't ever be there. Love and working out are similar in that way. You need to overcome an initial hesitation to get to the culminating goal.

The more love you make, the more love the Boyfriend Within will take, and give. Buckminster Fuller wrote somewhere that if you want to prevent highway accidents, you don't put up warning signs, you redesign the highway so that it's curved in such a way as to prevent accidents. In the following exercise we're thinking of ways in which you can build curves into your own personal highway to arrive at a more loving destination and to have a more loving and heartwarming trip getting there. While the notion of a warm heart might sound *merely* sentimental, it may well turn out in a study in a medical journal someday to exhibit positive biochemical results as well. But that's mostly just a guess on my part.

Awareness Exercise Fifteen

This exercise allows us to begin to design our own workout program for love. The first half is concerned with noticing how far you've come, perhaps without even keeping score. I don't know anyone who hasn't been practicing love in their lives to some extent. It seems to be an instinct. The second half of the exercise is concerned with devising new ways in which you can make room for even more love, and for its resulting advantages in your life.

To reflect the split agenda in this exercise, take a blank sheet of paper and draw a line down the middle. Label one side "Past" and the other side "Future." On the "Past" side, write down those times in your life when you've done extra work for love's sake. Your examples can be great or small, accidental or resolved, successful or overlooked. But I'm sure they're there. On my own list:

- Taking care of Howard when he was sick
- Helping a friend move

- Calling a sick acquaintance in the hospital
- Writing a thoughtful and explicit condolence card

Jumping out from the list in importance to me would be the first item: taking care of Howard when he was sick. Sickness and death are universal opportunities for care and service, of course. Certainly for gay men over the past decade, few calls have been more pressing than caring for those sick with AIDS. Especially during the earlier years of the medical crisis, the victims seemed cruelly fated to death camp–like horrors, some of which have been mitigated by developments in treatments since. I lived through one intense experience of caring. Many others—especially in New York City, Los Angeles, and San Francisco—have volunteered for a half dozen such cycles of rising and falling hopes and fears. And continue to do so.

Particularly relevant to this chapter is the payoff of such an experience and the realization of unexpected inner resources somehow made available for the task. I'm the type who, on principle, never would have volunteered for such service. Mother Teresa I'm not—and ten years ago, I was much less so. Almost every night before going to the hospital—during Howard's two lengthy hospital stays—I'd lie on my bed in my apartment having stomach cramps and a private tantrum before leaving. I just wanted to flee to a dirty movie theater, or to Palm Springs. And yet Howard maintained an astounding amount of wit and bravery. And our intimate capsule grew to be as fulfilling and satisfying as it could be stultifying, confining, and life stopping. The closer we came to death, the more on fire my heart seemed, and his, seemingly, as well. As a caregiver, I had direct experience of the paradox pointed to by the Voice: "Love makes you feel loved."

Now, on the second half of your page, labeled "Future," write down plans of action to experience this paradox of love if it isn't forced on you. For those who've been affected by the experience of being a caregiver, think how you can now seek out such opportunities so as not to lose what you gained. For those fortunate enough to have missed such a difficult lesson, think how you can begin to seek opportunities to exercise love in your own world. In these matters, remember, proportion is largely irrelevant. Small gestures can count as much as big. My own list of tactics on the "Future" side of my page includes:

- Follow my friend's example by making one nonbusiness call a day, a call based purely on love or friendship

- Give money on impulse to people or causes that move me—including tips to sympathetic waiters, cabdrivers
- Keep my ears tuned to people asking for favors, and consider saying yes rather than no automatically
- At least *reply* to unsolicited letters, gifts, invitations, rather than treating them as hostile interruptions

Most obvious to me in my "Future" list is its humbleness in scale compared to the "Past" list. But such humble goals can be rationalized. Love, or even simple kindness, is ambitious enough—the rewarding emotional honey coming after rather than before the experience. In place of the romantic model of fireworks, roses, and bells ringing, we have instead the less-seductive model of the frog that needs to be kissed to turn into a prince. That is, gratification is delayed. Works of love are matters of faith based on experience. So beginning small can be a good way to keep from being disappointed and put off early on. My own list of resolutions could be reduced to one simple theme: Bring down the wall!

•　　　•　　　•

GOING public follows naturally from private acts of love. It's the nature of love to want to find new expression. While I've been writing this, I've been watching out my window as two elderly gentlemen—one in a wheelchair—have been trying to flag down a taxi. Most of the yellow cabs simply whizzed past the problem situation. A few paused to consider the request before driving off. Finally one driver, who appeared to be of Caribbean origin, stopped to do the extra work of helping the two men into his cab, then loading the wheelchair into the trunk—before his meter could begin its ticking. A driver practiced in the ways of love would be much more likely to stop than one who wasn't yet in the groove. Like aerobics, or weight lifting, or dancing the night away, love is a learned habit.

The public expression of loving requires an even bigger step than the private expression. And the immediate emotional payback can be even more uncertain. In this case, trial and error is usually indicated. I was a member of an Episcopal parish in Manhattan for several years. One of my duties there was to feed the homeless—arriving early on Sunday morning to prepare tuna fish sandwiches, then standing on the steps of the church afterward to hand out the lunches to a line of obviously needy people. This was good and necessary work.

Personally, though, I've found the most visceral satisfaction in gay-related volunteerism. I think that the gay community has an advantage in being able to find opportunities for volunteering that are underexposed, personally stimulating, and implosive. If you're gay, and you travel to cities abroad, you have the chance to check into a local gay bar or café and meet locals in a way a straight tourist can't always manage as easily. Similarly in the sphere of volunteerism there are lots of activities, both intimate and communal, where you can see the benefits of whatever extra effort you make in ways often denied to those simply writing checks to support large causes such as finding a cure for cancer or muscular dystrophy—not that those causes can't offer heartwarming activities too, especially for those who've lost friends or family to one of these diseases.

Awareness Exercise Sixteen

List activities that are worthy and exciting *possibilities* for your own volunteerism, if and when you're ready. You may initially feel you don't have enough time. You may be pressured by an overload at work. But first just try to see how many possible activities you come up with. You might even invent a few not yet tried that you see a place for. The more personal your list, the more opportunity you'll have of finding an activity that's right for you. On my list:

- Join "The Next Generation," a mentoring program for gay and lesbian students at Columbia University
- Volunteer for one of the outreach programs at Hetrick-Martin Institute
- Give money to, or take part in, benefits for programs for AIDS research or care, such as CRIA (Community Research Initiative on AIDS) or God's Love We Deliver
- Start a monthly discussion group in my home on gay spirituality

I find it significant that two of the programs of interest to me are transgenerational. The chance to jump generations is special. Part of the kick of being a parent or teacher is being in touch with a new generation—learning the lingo, finding out what music or video game is popular, getting the satisfaction of sharing any bits of common sense or wisdom picked up over the years. For single people who aren't parents, haven't adopted, or don't have teaching jobs, this pleasure is harder to find. Programs that involve adults mentoring younger people provide a reliable dose of this kind of exchange. The emotional return can be immediate and up front. And of course the value for those to whom you're giving your time is obvious. It's an example of a kind of volunteerism that has special nurturing values for gays and lesbians.

The friend who turned me on to "The Next Generation" program, a spin-off of GHAP (the Gay Health Advocacy Project) at Columbia University, found its get-togethers of gay adults and college students as exciting for him as for the students. "It's great to have your experiences be of value to someone else," he explained. "And to let these kids know of the support network that's out there. Talking with them never felt patronizing to me. I was able to easily respect them. There was a mutual freshness to be offered." Certainly one of the surprises of hands-on volunteering, especially in service to others, is the constant discovery that the refreshment is so often, as my friend so naturally put it, "mutual."

The Hetrick-Martin Institute in New York City is custom-made for such hands-across-the-generations excitement and fulfillment. It's an appropriate spot for those whose nurturing urges are being cramped by a lifestyle of too much "me." This nonprofit social center and school serves lesbian, gay, bisexual, and transgender youth, including homeless youth, young people with HIV, and all youth coming to terms with their sexuality. Volunteers can't be counselors, but they help at the after-school Drop-In Center, or Project First Step, reaching out to teenagers on the streets of the city, half of whom are gay or lesbian, many surviving by exchanging sex for money. If your city or town doesn't have anything of the sort, you might want to consider starting your own outreach to gay teens.

I dropped a "spiritual" activity into my own list because, ironically, I feel convinced that gays and lesbians—so often trashed by Christian fundamentalist groups—form one of the natural communities with a talent for ministry, liturgy, and an updating and deepening of spiritual life in this country, both for themselves and others. There's certainly a long tradition of single priests, nuns, prophets, shamans, and church organists to be tapped. I think that gays have particular promise for cultivating a new orchid of spiritual life, a successful hybrid, as long as it's attached to a plant rooted without denial in the black, erotic soil they've tilled so generously over the past few decades. Certainly everyone's Boyfriend Within has much to teach about how to proceed in such sincere and invisible matters.

Few parties are more exuberant than the Morning Party held yearly on Fire Island, each year's splash more extravagant, costumed, populated, and "done" than the last. I'm all for morning parties . . . as well as afternoon parties, evening parties, midnight dips, and so on. There can never be enough. But I did have a thought while staring out into that tanned crowd so full of energy, life, and blatant financial and creative resources: "What would it be like to take all of the time, planning, and fire that went into this one day and focus it, as rays through a magnifying glass, onto other kinds of activity?" There's definitely a tremendous amount of energy in the gay community that has yet to be used and exploited, certainly in "selfless" service in activities that will hopefully continue on past the immediate crisis of AIDS. My perception wasn't a put-down of the summer holiday's joy—just a quick vision of something else, of extra possibilities.

Of course the Boyfriend Within responds to all heartfelt contributing, regardless of the sexual orientataion and gender of the recipient(s). He's an equal-opportunity lover. Gay issues might have a special resonance for some, but not for all. If your heart is somewhere else, then that's where you're probably going to want to look to experiment. Again, churches, synagogues, and mosques have the longest association with such voluntary labor—*seva* is a Hindu word, but hardly an exclusively Hindu activity. There are plenty of programs to choose from in every denomination—gays now even have their own denomination, the Metropolitan Community Church, which has its headquarters in Los Angeles. Political activity counts too. If you feel expansive marching at the Washington Mall for a larger cause, go *there*. Some art lovers feel fulfilled by volunteering to give tours at museums; book lovers by helping at the library. Satisfying options are as varied as are Boyfriends Within.

The key concept of chapter 3, on dating the Boyfriend Within, was, "To get to know the Boyfriend Within, you have to get outside yourself." This paradox has only been further unfolded in this chapter, beginning again with paradoxes from the Voice: "Love is . . . work. Love makes you feel loved." Volunteering is a comprehensive gesture of this understanding. We get to know and develop our relationship with the Boyfriend Within by actions—not by thoughts, words, whims, or moods. We need to make time and space if we are really to pass through the life changes made possible by this felt connection. Volunteerism can simply be thought of as the most fulfilling of dates with the Boyfriend Within. It's the one date that's guaranteed to be purely and simply about love.

Awareness Exercises:

15   Draw a line down the middle of a blank sheet of paper. Label one side "Past" and the other "Future." On the "Past" side write down those times in your life when you've done extra work for love's sake. On the "Future" side write down future possibilities for such good deeds in your own social circle.

16.   List activities in the larger world that are worthy and exciting possibilities for your own volunteerism.

CONCLUSION

No one has written more beautifully or intricately about the Boyfriend Within than the thirteenth-century Persian poet Rumi. For several years, he'd experienced an intense friendship with a wandering dervish, Shams of

Tabriz, with whom he spent days and months at a stretch, talking and sharing late-night sessions of music, song, and dance. One day, however, Shams simply disappeared. Rumi, devastated by the loss, traveled to Damascus to search for his dear friend. In Damascus, he had an insight that altered his life and transformed him into one of the world's great poets:

> *Why should I seek? I am the same as*
> *he. His essence speaks through me.*
> *I have been looking for myself!*

In an introduction to *The Essential Rumi*, his translator appropriately capitalized both the words "Friend" and "Friendship" whenever referring to the beloved Shams.

Mystical poetry might have the reputation of concerning itself with flights of imagination or heightened experience not available to the ordinary person—the man in the Gap flannel shirt, as it were. Certainly anything thirteenth-century, Persian, or Islamic could excusably be thought exotic enough to put back on the shelf, slightly out of reach. But in fact Rumi in his thousands of poems describes the very experience of finding a Boyfriend Within, and his experience is available to anyone. In some people's lives, such transformation comes about seemingly without even trying. Chalk it up as one of life's lessons. In most cases, however, personal change requires help and takes time.

Hopefully by now you've encountered your own Boyfriend Within. We're all traveling from different directions yet can choose to arrive, finally, at a similar place—the place described by Rumi as "of Friend and friend." I was moved by the loss of a lover to AIDS and by a personal bout of self-questioning. Others have arrived at the same spot earlier or later in their lives, or they have gotten there out of quite different predicaments. I had lunch recently with someone I went to college with who's been in an open yet profound and binding relationship with his lover for twenty-five years. On the side, he dallied with several lightweight romances. But he confessed he'd lost his energy and enthusiasm for such thin mirages. He and his lover have been trying to learn to live with themselves in order to live more successfully with each other. This friend and I had reached some similar conclusions about sex and romance: he, "married"; I, single.

My own initial casting about was motivated by longing. I was longing for a lost friend, our relationship made more idyllic by the passing of time. I was longing, too, to meet a new provider of security, comfort, and happiness—a replacement. Such longing is hardly unusual. I find longing, more than any other theme, permeates gay poetry and fiction. Certainly this longing has been the motor of much human romance, love, politics, and history. But the actions and beliefs arising out of the feeling are not necessarily fixed and determined.

At the risk of sounding like a poor man's twelve-step program, this path of self-transformation I've outlined does have its own logic. If you've worked through the chapters and Awareness Exercises in this book, many of the discoveries and insights are behind you. And yet they are also ahead. For as you continue to consult the Voice—which for me has become a daily habit—and as you return to relevant sections of this book, you're free to mix and match discussions and exercises according to your own needs. It's helpful, though, to try to keep the entire scaffolding in mind.

Chapter 1 on "Why don't I have a boyfriend?" is a meditation on some of the wishes, lies, and dreams that follow from initial longing. Here we get a chance to locate the feeling of longing where it lives—within us. And we begin to locate its antidote of happiness and satisfaction within as well. The chapter is centered on demystifying the power of "boyfriend" as crutch, illusion, or confining role in our lives. Whether we're single or involved, this insight can free us up to begin to look within ourselves and outward to the world in a fresh way.

Chapter 2—"Who *is* the Boyfriend Within?"— brings the personal responsibility for finding our own Boyfriend Within into this work of self-discovery. Such work must necessarily be interactive because everyone's Boyfriend Within is slightly different, as is the unique combination of everyone's body type, blood type, perhaps astrological sign, and certainly genetic code. Some need peace and nurturing from their BFW. Others need permission to be wild and creative. Still others need adrenaline, a shot in the arm. This getting-to-know-you phase is active and introspective.

Chapter 3 on "How do I get to know the Boyfriend Within?" introduces the notion of dating. The real movement begins here, the back and forth, or "call and response." It's as if you've become a dance partner with yourself. The Boyfriend Within becomes not simply a notion, a catchy phrase, or even a feeling or a resolution. Time spent with the Boyfriend Within includes all the ups and downs, tugs and pulls of a dating cycle with a new friend. You need to make time and space. You need to commit.

Chapter 4 deals with the flip side: "What if I'm

having problems with my Boyfriend Within?" The Boyfriend Within is a blessing and an enhancement, but not a painkiller. He's unfortunately not psychic Prozac. And the choice to be sensitive to messages from within, like all human choices, must be considered as fitful and subject to change. We're still going to get the blues. There are times when we'd rather just shut down and suffer. Remember: We're adjusting our orientation here, not trading in our genus and species.

These interior adjustments wouldn't matter much if they didn't create changes in the way we live. Chapter 5—"How does the Boyfriend Within relate to a Boyfriend Without?"—considers some of the repercussions when dealing with others. Whether single, married, or dating, we all bring a host of expectations to the table. Consciously learning to locate our center of gravity within creates a personal revolution. We no longer require of our mates all sorts of inappropriate behavior for which they're not suited, or on which they haven't even been briefed. And we no longer look at being single as necessarily a lack, or failure. We learn to deal alertly with the world as it is, not as we think it should be. Formulaic scripts are tossed.

Chapter 6—"What's love got to do with it?"—presents one of the core concepts which can grow out of a deeper experience of the Boyfriend Within. We're used to thinking of love in romantic terms. Love is usually experienced as a sweet burning in the heart, accompanied by a great sense of well-being and self-satisfaction. Love makes us feel good about ourselves. But one of the mysteries of life is the way in which doing work (or "selfless service") for people we care about, or causes we care about, can also make our hearts burn within us. We can literally create the afterglow of love in ourselves by going on dates of personally meaningful volunteerism with the Boyfriend Within.

A great boon of the love and intimacy experienced in a good relationship, or in a functional family, is a *release* from some of the pain, stress, and alienation of our lives. To "come home" is to let down your guard a little, take off your tie, kick off your shoes, and let slip the mask, or masks, of persona applied during the day. But of course home is wherever you choose. You can turn your office into a temporary home by shutting the door and watching the sunset. Or your car, when you're driving along listening to a favorite book on tape.

Similarly you can create love and intimacy wherever you want. You can do so by learning to access your relationship to the Boyfriend Within. As the saying goes, home is where you hang your hat. Love and happiness can be found whenever, wherever, and however you allow yourself release from bad feelings, impermanent constraints, or contrived behavior. Some sessions will take more time and more unwinding; others, less.

A few weeks ago I visited a younger friend in the East Village. During a lull while he was changing a Metallica tape on his malfunctioning boom box, I eavesdropped on a couple of his twenty-something roommates discussing girl troubles in the next room. One of them said, "Well, my number one rule in dealing with women is just be yourself. I mean you can be a little bit more polite or more thoughtful than usual. But basically be yourself." His cliché rang through to me as so innocent . . . but also so inspiring, so true. He was the mouthpiece at that moment for a wise truth about dealing with the Boyfriend (or in his case, Girlfriend) Without.

I rediscovered the application of this truth for the Boyfriend Within for the dozenth time a few nights later. I'd had one of those days. It was late. I knew that to get my seven hours I needed to get to bed soon. But I was still churning, still having an imaginary conversation with an annoying magazine editor, and I was vexed about a trip that wasn't gelling. Luckily I decided to take some time for the Inner B: I put on

Chant; relaxed under a blanket on the couch, in a room lit by only a single candle. Within a half hour I was a happy camper. My worries were thankfully reduced to an appropriate scale of silly insignificance. I'd even figured out a structure for my next book, which had been eluding me for months. That is: I released *myself.* And I had done so by giving myself time and permission to just be myself, with myself. I'd adapted the twenty-something's advice for my own purposes.

I'm not saying that by bringing the Boyfriend Within into the conscious center of our lives we'll be *entirely* content. I have no idea where rich and successful fit into the picture, though I hope they're part of it. But I do believe that when we learn to find our Boyfriends Within, our hearts will become less restless. We'll tend to be happier.

In the words of Rumi: "Lovers don't finally meet somewhere / They're in each other all along."

W9-BRX-166

HEART
TROUBLE

Books in the Woman's Workshop Series

Woman's Workshop Series

HEART TROUBLE

STUDIES ON CHRISTIAN CHARACTER

BARBARA BUSH

Lamplighter Books Grand Rapids, Michigan
Zondervan Publishing House

Heart Trouble: A Woman's Workshop on Christian Character

Requests for information should be addressed to:
Zondervan Publishing House
Grand Rapids, Michigan 49530

Copyright © 1985 by Barbara Bush
Grand Rapids, Michigan

Library of Congress Cataloging in Publication Data

Bush, Barbara.
    Heart trouble.
    (A Lamplighter book)
1. Christian life—1960– 2. Women—Religious life. I. Title.
BV4501.2.B92   1985   248.8'43'076   85-5311
ISBN 0-310-29431-2

Madame Camille Monet and a Child in a Garden by Claude Monet
Cover Photo by SUPERSTOCK INTERNATIONAL
Cover Design by *The Church Art Works*, Salem, Oregon

All rights reserved. No part of this publication may be reproduced, stored in a retrieval system, or transmitted in any form or by any means—electronic, mechanical, photocopy, recording, or any other—except for brief quotations in printed reviews, without the prior permission of the publisher.

Printed in the United States of America

92 93 94 95 96 / CH / 18 17 16 15 14

Listen to me, everyone, and understand this. Nothing outside a man can make him "unclean" by going into him. Rather, it is what comes out of a man that makes him "unclean." . . . For from within, out of men's hearts, come evil thoughts, sexual immorality, theft, murder, adultery, greed, malice, deceit, lewdness, envy, slander, arrogance and folly. All these evils come from inside and make a man "unclean."

Mark 7:14, 21–23

CONTENTS

SUGGESTIONS FOR GROUP USE

Choose a meeting place suitable to the type and size of your group. This can be a Sunday school classroom or home or elsewhere. If the group is to meet in a home, try to find one other than that of the leader. A hostess may have difficulty turning people out of her own home when class is over, but the leader can encourage group members to leave on time by leaving promptly herself. You will find it is easier to secure a hostess if she knows people will leave promptly.

Set a time schedule for class sessions and stick to it faithfully. If coffee or other refreshments are served (this is not a necessity), include this in the schedule, but be sure that the lesson period starts and ends on time. It is the leader's responsibility to keep faith with group members in the matter of time.

Approach each phase of building a study group prayerfully. Pray that God will guide your decisions, bring the right women to your group, give you wisdom as you study the material, give you love for each woman, and open each heart to His truth.

The leader may want to open each lesson with a summary of the character traits studied so far. Class members may share current items relating to the study from newspaper or magazine articles or other books. During group discussion the leader should keep things moving so that all questions are covered by the end of the allotted time.

Draw quiet women into the discussion whenever possible. You may ask them to answer specific questions so that more talkative women do not overpower them. However, questions that are more personal in nature (as opposed to those that have a specific answer from Scripture) should be answered only by volunteers. In addition to the printed questions, the leader might ask, "Which part of the chapter interested you most?" or "Which question was the most thought-provoking?"

Encourage the women to personalize the week's topic so that the study does not become merely an intellectual exercise. Close each class session with an opportunity for group members to commit some area of their lives to the Lord. If they would like to share with the group what that commitment is, they should be encouraged to do so, but no one should feel pressured to make a public statement. The leader may use questions such as the following:

Has the lesson revealed a specific area in your life that needs attention?

Have you discovered a problem in your life relating to a particular character trait?

Is the Lord prodding you to take some action, to obey Him in some specific way?

The leader should then close in a prayer of dedication.

Getting the Group Started

This book can be used by individuals as well as in group situations. A group should plan to meet for twelve weeks so that the first session can be used to get acquainted, pass out materials, and get organized.

The first session is a good time to set a few friendly ground rules. These might include:

1. We will keep to our schedule, starting and ending on time.

2. We are asked to commit ourselves to prepare for each session by: studying thoroughly the assigned chapter and answering all the "Digging Deeper" questions. (Some groups set a rule that no one may discuss a question without a written answer. This helps eliminate "off the top of the head" and unscriptural answers that can sidetrack the discussion.)

3. During discussion, unless the question calls for a personal opinion, we will avoid statements that start with "I think" or "I feel." Instead, we will try to share what God is saying in the Bible.

4. We will keep private information within the group. We will use information to pray for one another and the leader.

Topical studies such as this one encounter special problems when group members use different versions of the Bible. Biblical quotations in the text of this study are generally from the New International Version. The leader will need to be alert to any confusion caused when differing key words describing character traits are used in various translations. You may want to encourage the women to use versions other than the Living Bible, since it is a paraphrase with substantially different wording than major Bible translations. Encourage the women to keep their Bibles open during discussion so that versions and answers can be compared without wasting time.

1

HEART TROUBLE

A major television network recently presented a program about what type of person is most susceptible to heart attacks. Included in the program was a test for viewers to score themselves, based on age, weight, sex, diet, habits, and physical condition. When the points were added, each viewer knew what his or her potential for heart trouble was.

Cardiovascular problems are much discussed these days, and people with high blood pressure and elevated cholesterol counts are watched closely. But many of us have heart disease of a different kind, and we are not receiving any warnings at all. We are in spiritual rather than physical jeopardy, and often we are not even aware of it.

Jeremiah tells us that it is difficult even to diagnose our spiritual problems because our natural reaction is to keep our symptoms hidden, even from ourselves. ''The heart is more deceitful than all else and is desperately sick; who can understand it?" (Jer. 17:9, NASB). Just as smokers tell themselves that they will never face lung cancer, or junk food lovers ignore warnings about their health, many of us reassure ourselves that our spiritual lives are fine even when we don't feel very well inside. And just as some people avoid doctors, we refuse to look for help because we are afraid to find out that something is wrong.

In March, 1980, in Washington, scientists noticed that Mount St. Helens was beginning to make some ominous sounds beneath the surface. As the mountain began emitting plumes of smoke and earthquakes occurred, authorities evacuated the area and closed off nearby highways. Some long-time residents refused to leave; one or two geologists took up posts within the area to observe the phenomenon more closely; a few campers strayed into the area, either uninformed of the danger or doubtful of it.

But the eruption did come on May 18 with a force five hundred times greater than the atomic bomb dropped on Hiroshima. The resulting blast of searing heat, molten lava, steam, rock, and ash left seventy-five persons dead, the entire mountain rearranged, trees snapped, and automobiles squashed. Glaciers melted, sending torrents of water and mud coursing down to the valleys, and pumice and dust were showered on towns 450 miles away.

The spiritual human heart can be compared to a volcano like Mount St. Helens. Before trouble starts, everything may look fine on the outside. Perhaps a little steam let off here, a rumble there, but nothing we feel we can't handle. However, just as a beautiful mountain can become a wasteland in minutes, so our lives can be ruined by the words and deeds that issue from unrepentant, neglected hearts.

Finding Spiritual Health

Our physical bodies do not become strong unless we put the necessary ingredients into them. People whose diets lack vital nutrients end up with stunted growth, malfunctioning organs, and even brain damage. Our spiritual lives do not progress without proper care, either. This growth is sometimes referred to as our "sanctification," our increase in holiness, becoming more like Christ. We grow as we increase in the knowledge of God and His principles for our lives, as we develop Christian character.

When we receive Jesus Christ as our Savior, we are born into God's family (John 1:12). But the Bible tells us we are like babies and need to take scriptural nourishment to mature. "Like newborn babies, crave pure spiritual milk, so that by it you may grow up in your salvation" (1 Peter 2:2). Some growth is easy and rather painless, some comes only after much trial and tears. That is because some changes in our conduct are surface changes, while others demand excavations into the bedrock of our hardened natures.

Levels of Growth

If a woman had a Christian upbringing, some aspects of Christian character undoubtedly were encouraged from birth. Her *habits* are a help rather than a hindrance as she starts to explore the levels of Christian growth.

Even for someone with no Christian background, some habits are easy to change for the new Christian. Instead of sleeping in on Sunday, getting to church each week is often a joy. Foul language may disappear instantly from the daily vocabulary. Sometimes even the desire to continue more harmful habits dies at the moment of salvation, though this is not always the case.

The next level of growth in Christian character, *actions*, may be a little harder to change. Often we know what the right behavior is but fail to follow through; or we realize we should not participate in some activity, but do so anyway. Sometimes much time and study are required before a person grasps the biblical principles that guide the Christian in proper behavior.

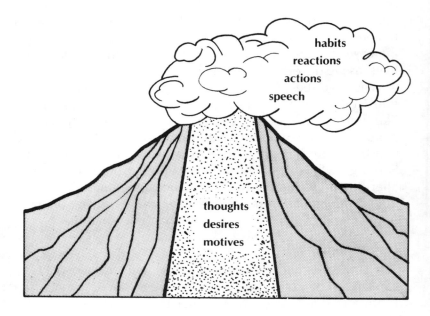

It is even more difficult to control our *reactions*. Someone surprises us with a question we don't want to answer, and we lie. Another car collides with our car, and we blow a fuse. A customer gives us a hard time, and we respond sarcastically. We may be able to keep ourselves in hand when things go smoothly, but sudden stress reveals character flaws.

At another level yet, our *speech* may betray heart problems of which we are not even conscious. Envy or self-centeredness can be unknowingly revealed by our everyday conversations. Questionable language and stories, angry or bitter turns of phrase, or whining tones of voice show others the spiritual battles still unwon.

Habits, actions, and speech are all on the surface, displayed in our daily living to any who want to find out if our conduct matches our professed beliefs. But hidden at yet deeper levels are our *desires*, our *thoughts*, our *motives*, unseen and unknown by anyone until they express themselves in word or deed.

Our concern for spiritual progress—our realized need for growth in Christian character—cannot be limited to those levels where other people can see, for God probes the depths of our souls and holds us responsible for what He finds there. We cannot fool Him, for the Bible assures us that "the LORD does not look at the things man looks at. Man looks at the outward appearance, but the LORD looks at the heart" (1 Sam. 16:7). We may think we are doing pretty well compared to others we know. But Proverbs 16:2 warns: "All a man's ways seem innocent to him, but motives are weighed by the LORD." And God told Jeremiah, "I the LORD search the heart and examine the mind, to reward a man according to his conduct, according to what his deeds deserve" (Jer. 17:10).

If we feel that God is satisfied with us so long as our outward behavior is circumspect, we run a high risk of heart trouble. We are like the people who watched the program about heart attacks and didn't heed its findings. Such people may have arteries in bad shape, but they can't see them, so they blithely go on their way. Jesus said our behavior will sooner or later begin to reveal our inner condition: "For from within, out of men's hearts, come evil thoughts, sexual immorality, theft, murder, adultery, greed, malice, deceit, lewdness, envy, slander, arrogance and folly. All these evils come from inside and make a man 'unclean'" (Mark 7:21—23).

If we do not want ourselves and our loved ones defiled by such evils, we must take seriously our inner lacks in Christian character. We must ask ourselves how much we have really progressed in the secret areas of our lives, whether we are more Christlike than we were a year ago, or when we first professed our faith in Christ. If not, we must come to God in confession and prayer, and ask that not only the words of our mouths, but also the meditations of our hearts might be pleasing in God's sight (Ps. 19:14).

DIGGING DEEPER

1. Why is it foolish to try to ignore our heart problems (1 Chronicles 28:9)? _____

_____

_____

_____

2. Do you know any people who are "walking volcanoes," ready to erupt at any time? How do you feel around them? _____

_____

_____

_____

3. Do people have to treat you carefully to keep you from "boiling over" or "spouting off"? If so, what does that indicate about your spiritual condition? _____

_____

_____

_____

4. What does "sanctification" mean? Read Hebrews 9:13–14 in light of the volcano illustration. Then find a Bible dictionary definition. _____

_____

_____

_____

5. Read 1 Corinthians 10:1—12 to find out the following:

   a. Despite all the spiritual riches the Israelites experienced (verses 1—4), what was God's opinion of His people (verse 5)? _____

_____

   b. What specific sins are mentioned (verses 7—10)?

_____

_____

   c. Why were these episodes recorded (verses 6, 11)?

_____

_____

   d. What warning are we given (verse 12)? _____

_____

   e. How does this warning relate to Jeremiah 17:9 and this chapter on "Heart Trouble"? _____

_____

_____

   f. What spiritual riches have been given to Christians today? _____

_____

_____

g. How well do you stand up to your "wilderness experiences"? _____

_____

h. What were God's judgments on those Jews? How should this affect Christians (Romans 11:21)?_____

_____

_____

6. On the other hand, what promise does God give (Jeremiah 29:13; Matthew 5:6)?_____

_____

_____

_____

7. On which levels are most of your spiritual battles fought: habits, actions, reactions, speech, desires, thoughts, motives? _____

_____

_____

_____

8. With which areas of your life would the Lord not be pleased? _____

_____

_____

_____

2

A CLEAN HEART

Create in me a clean heart, O God, and renew a steadfast spirit within me (Ps. 51:10, NASB).

When we look honestly at ourselves during this study and see how far short we fall of the Christian character God desires, we may be upset. But our distress does not need to last. First, because God isn't finished with our growth process. "He who began a good work in you will carry it on to completion until the day of Christ Jesus" (Phil. 1:6).

Second, because, if we discover our character falls short because of our wrong choices, there is a solution. In Romans 3:23 we learn that God's term for "falling short" is "sin." And while we may not know what to do in every situation, Christians should know what to do about sin. 1 John 1:9 says, "If we confess our sins, he is faithful and just and will forgive us our sins and purify us from all unrighteousness."

What a relief that is! Just as we could admit to some physical disease if we knew a simple procedure would cure it, so we can risk getting a spiritual cardiogram because the remedy for every malady is already known. At any cost, however, we must expose our shortcomings to the light, because our sins have several serious side effects.

Sin Is Contagious

First, sin, like many infections, spreads (Rom. 5:12). The effect of Adam's and Eve's sins spread so quickly that one son murdered another. And though we may not like to admit it, *our* sin affects others also. Our families bear the brunt of our unloving behavior. We transmit unholy attitudes to our children. Even total strangers can be affected.

When Mount St. Helens exploded, thousands of people, some living as far as two hundred miles away, suffered from the results. People sometimes like to say, "This is my life and it's no one's business what I do." This attempt to alleviate guilt does not alter the truth that virtually all of our actions affect someone else for good or ill. Certainly our character deficiencies make life less pleasant for those who have to deal with us.

I can still remember vividly a train trip my family took in the 1950's from California to Lansing, Michigan. The last leg of our journey was accomplished by chair car on a night train from Chicago to Lansing. In the sparsely populated coach, an obviously inebriated man up front was a source of fascination to my sister and me. We watched him sway back and forth in his seat for an hour or two, then get to his feet and begin lurching toward us up the aisle on his way to the restroom. Just as he drew even with our family, his time came, and he threw up, some of his deposit landing on my father's suit. I can still hear my dad's voice: "Oh, no, it's none of my business if he drinks, oh, no! His drinking is his affair! He can throw up all over me, but it's none of my business!"

Others have suffered in far more devastating and permanent ways from the actions of others; some have even lost their lives. Eve did not mean for her disobedience (after all, she only plucked one piece of fruit) to have such a wide-ranging effect. Nevertheless, sin causes pain, and its infection spreads unless checked by supernatural means.

Direct victims are not the only ones affected by sin; observers are also touched by it. Children see a father cheating in a business deal or a mother gossiping, and they adopt the same behavior. One couple in a group of friends divorces, and before long several others follow suit. Young couples know of others who are living together unmarried and decide to join the trend. A child sees a parent turn to liquor in times of stress and copies that habit. The sins of the children, however, need not mirror their parents' exactly: Eve's sin was disobedience—Cain's was murder.

In the course of our lives, how many people do we touch and influence? Are others encouraged by our actions to moral living, or tempted to try to get away with something?

Sin Compounds

David, despite his unique knowledge and experience of God, apparently did not foresee any grave complications when he committed adultery with Bathsheba (2 Sam. 11). As king he was accustomed to getting what he wanted, and he wanted Bathsheba. But to keep his disobedience to God from being revealed, David finally ordered the death of Uriah, Bathsheba's husband.

The lie we tell may seem an isolated instance. But often we end up having to deny we lied, digging ourselves deeper into a hole. We can even begin implicating others, asking them to lie for us. A president of the United States was forced to resign from office because he tried to cover up (and to force others to help conceal) a comparatively minor criminal act in which he apparently was not even initially involved!

It is a common misconception that sin exists singly in people. We say, "He is a wonderful person who just drinks too much," or, ". . . who enjoys the homosexual lifestyle." We tell ourselves, "I am a good Christian with only this one fault."

On the contrary, each sin we allow in ourselves makes it easier for us to allow others. If people will steal, they will not balk at lying; it is foolish to look for honor among thieves. A woman who cheats on her husband will not be a trustworthy friend either. We do, indeed, weave "a tangled web" when we first decide to deceive.

Sin Is Deadly

David's sin with Bathsheba resulted in death not only for Uriah, but also for the infant born of the union. Samson's inability to put God before Delilah's charms caused him to become his enemies's slave and eventually claimed his life.

When the Bible says, "The wages of sin is death" (Rom. 6:23), and "The soul who sins will die" (Ezek. 18:4, NASB), our minds often picture only the most heinous acts deserving such punishment. But the Bible clearly states that whoever "stumbles at just one point is guilty of breaking all" of the Law (James 2:10). In other words, a miss is as good as a mile. Our "smaller" sins are as death-inducing as our "larger" ones. Eve's sin of disbelief earned the same judgment as murder: "You will surely die" (Gen. 2:17). It is sin itself that causes the disintegration, not the particular manifestation of it.

The death spoken of is not necessarily immediately physical. We may first find that our character flaws have killed a relationship or destroyed a reputation. Or perhaps we will so ignore our inner promptings that our consciences die.

God's Cure-All

The good news for our heart trouble is that God does not deal in Band-aids but in miraculous recoveries—the miracle of complete healing for all the wounds of sin. We can dare to turn out even the dark corners of our hearts because Jesus has already paid the penalty for whatever we find there. He has "surely died" instead of us. We can admit, "I am a bitter, unforgiving woman . . . I am greedy and jealous of the good fortune of others . . . I am an alcoholic . . . or adulteress." For "He was pierced for our transgressions, he was crushed for our iniquities; the punishment that brought us peace was upon him, and by his wounds we are healed" (Isa. 53:5).

We hide our faults at our own peril, as does the patient who tells the physician only half of her symptoms. If we want total healing, we must watch diligently for whatever God might point out as causing infection. As a wound must be thoroughly cleansed to heal properly, so our hearts need this same attention.

> Cleanse me with hyssop, and I will be clean; wash me, and I will be whiter than snow. . . . Create in me a pure heart, O God.   Psalm 51:7, 10

The Reality of Cleansing

King David stands as a prime example not only of sin but also of the reality of forgiveness. His character, which had stood up so admirably under the tremendous injustice and insane jealousy of Saul, faltered at one crucial point in his life. As a result, he misused his power as king and committed adultery with the wife of an officer who was even then off defending king and country. He then slyly called Uriah home, encouraging him to go see his wife overnight, hoping to have his sin covered. But Uriah was so dedicated to David and his duty that he refused to indulge himself while his cohorts still fought. This loyalty sealed his doom. David sent a message back by Uriah's own hand telling his captain to put Uriah in the front line of battle and then withdraw, assuring his death. The betrayals of godly character seem too numerous to count; the sordid story would seem surely to constitute the end of David's glory.

But what is God's final opinion of David? Years after David's death, God said of him, his heart was "fully devoted to the LORD his God" (1 Kings 11:4). What an epitaph! How could this be after all of David's sins?

The answer lies in Psalm 51, David's prayer of repentance. To read this psalm is to enter into the distress of a soul acknowledging sin without rationalization or excuse, casting itself wholly upon God's mercy, a "broken and contrite heart" pleading for cleansing.

David's story proves that our sins, no matter how repugnant, need not separate us permanently from God and His plan for us. The path back to Him lies in the complete repentance mirrored in Psalm 51. The restoration to fellowship with God results not from a half-hearted "forgive me," but a broken spirit.

God specializes in miracle cures, and we, as well as David, can be known as those "fully devoted to the Lord our God," no matter how serious our character lapses, or sins, may be. God knows how to make clean hearts out of dirty ones. Praise Him!

DIGGING DEEPER

1. How did God show the seriousness of various kinds of sins?

a. Genesis 2:16–17. Was this judgment carried out immediately? How was it accomplished (3:22–24)? _____

_____

_____

b. Leviticus 24:16–17, 23. Was this judgment carried out immediately? _____

_____

_____

c. Numbers 16:1–2, 31–33. Was this judgment carried out immediately? _____

_____

_____

2. Why are we sometimes careless about our sins (Psalm 10:13; 2 Peter 3:3–4)? _____

_____

_____

3. What should we understand (Isaiah 48:9; 2 Peter 3:9)?

_____

_____

4. Why will Christians never have to face God's wrath and judgment for their sins (Romans 5:8–9; 8:1–2; 1 Peter 2:24)?_____

_____

_____

5. What will the Christian have to face (Romans 14:12)? How does this knowledge affect you? _____

_____

_____

_____

_____

6. How does God intend the thought of coming before His greatness to affect us (Exodus 20:18–20)? _____

_____

_____

_____

7. Are there things in your life that used to bother your conscience but no longer do? What could that indicate (Hebrews 3:13)? _____

_____

_____

_____

8. How does a dirty heart affect your prayer life (Psalm 66:18; Isaiah 1:15, 16)?_____

_____

_____

9. What is Jesus' standard for your character (Matthew 5:48)? "Perfect" here means to "grow into complete maturity of godliness in mind and character" (Amplified Bible). _____

_____

Scan the following and list the areas of conduct to which Jesus applied this standard.

    a. Matthew 5:21–22 _____

    b. 5:27–28 _____

    c. 5:31–32 _____

    d. 5:33–37 _____

e. 5:38–41 _____

f. 5:43–44 _____

Assign one or more of the following to the above Scripture passages: habit, action, reaction, speech, desire, thought, motive.

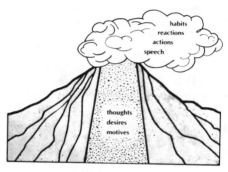

10. What is often our standard for behavior (Luke 18:11)?

_____

11. If we saw our hearts as God sees, what would be our attitude (Psalm 40:12; Isaiah 6:5)? _____

_____

12. How can our hearts and consciences be cleansed (Hebrews 9:13, 14)? _____

_____

13. How clean does God promise to get our hearts (1 John 1:7, 9)? _____

_____

14. Make a list of as many sins as God reveals to you. Read Psalm 51 aloud as your personal prayer of repentance and restoration.

3

A HUMBLE HEART

Take my yoke upon you and learn from me, for I am gentle and humble in heart, and you will find rest for your souls (Matt. 11:29).

Christians have speculated for centuries about why God chose Mary to bear the Messiah. Yes, it was "the fullness of time" in God's great plan; certainly a young Jewish woman was needed. But the birth had to take place in Bethlehem. So why Mary of Nazareth?

Perhaps the answer can be found if we analyze Mary's own words as she expressed her feelings to Elizabeth:

My soul glorifies the Lord and my spirit rejoices in God my Savior,

for he has been mindful of the humble state of his servant . . .

for the Mighty One has done great things for me— holy is his name. . . .

He has scattered those who are proud in their inmost thoughts.

He has brought down rulers from their thrones but has
lifted up the humble.
He has filled the hungry with good things but has sent
the rich away empty.   Luke 1:46–53

Clearly, Mary saw in God's choice the proof that He favors
the humble over the proud. She apparently knew of no other
qualification for God's choosing her. She said, "All generations will call me blessed" only because "the Mighty One
has done great things for me" (Luke 1:48–49).

The Meaning of Humility

Many people find it hard to understand what it means to
be humble. They may think of a humble person as someone
who sits quietly in a corner, never opening her mouth or
making her presence known. This is not God's view. How
would His work get done if everyone sat in a corner? Who
would greet the stranger? Who would reach out to the
hurting? Who would teach His Word? Humility is not
shyness or even quietness. The humble woman is one who
appreciates herself, but whose recognition of her own
shortcomings keeps her from being proud, who submits to
authority, and who respects other people as having much
worth to add to her life.

Mary was no shrinking violet. She did not hesitate to
question an angel (Luke 1:34), and she verbalized her
feelings easily (verses 46–55). She traveled from Galilee to
Judah in the early weeks of her pregnancy and repeated the
journey when it was time to deliver. She endured the danger
attendant to Jesus' birth (Matt. 2:13–15), and lived in a
foreign country for years before returning to Nazareth. She
appears even to have established a natural relationship with
her very unusual Son (Luke 2:42–51; John 2:1–5) while
caring for at least six other children (Mark 6:3). She endured

the agony of seeing her Son crucified, and became an active member of the early church (Acts 1:13–14). These are not the accomplishments of a timid, diffident person, yet Mary is described as humble.

Moses was one of the greatest leaders the world has known. Yet we are told, "Now Moses was a very humble man, more humble than anyone else on the face of the earth" (Num. 12:3). Jesus said, "I am gentle and humble in heart" (Matt. 11:29). Obviously, humility does not correlate with lack of ability or confidence, or a colorless personality.

As with many character traits in this study, humility may best be understood by comparing it with its opposite. Several times the Bible says, "God opposes the proud but gives grace to the humble" (Prov. 3:34; James 4:6; 1 Peter 5:5). The humble, then, are those who continually guard themselves against the sin of pride. In Romans 12, Paul has several specific suggestions to help us. He does not say we are to think poorly of ourselves to be humble but rather, "Do not think of yourself more highly than you *ought,*. . . with sober judgment" (verse 3, emphasis mine). This, he says, regardless of whether our task in the church is serving, teaching, contributing to the needs of others, leading, or showing mercy (verses 6–8). In addition, he counsels:

> Live in harmony with one another. Do not be proud, but be willing to associate with people of low position. Do not be conceited. Do not repay anyone evil for evil. . . . As far as it depends on you, live at peace with everyone. Do not take revenge, my friends . . . (verses 16–19).

The humble, then, are to be active in the Lord's work— ministering to others rather than sitting on the sidelines waiting for others to minister to them. They are not to feel self-important, but like Mary they are to realize that their very ability to serve God is a gift from Him, "the measure of faith God has given you" (Rom. 12:3).

People who live like smoldering volcanoes, getting their feelings hurt, harboring resentment and bitterness because of slights or lack of recognition, or seeking ways to get back at others, are not humble people, no matter how quiet their basic personalities may be. The truly humble need not be handled "with kid gloves." It is pride, not humility, that causes us to take offense easily. For our own sake and for the sake of those whom we encounter, God would have us deal with our sin.

The Humble Are Teachable

One of the most obvious ways to identify the humble is to look for the desire to learn more of God's truth. The self-righteous, proud woman does not like to admit she needs anything, and she dislikes the role of learner. But the humble woman realizes she is "poor in spirit" (Matt. 5:3) and needs instruction from the Lord.

Those who parade their Bible knowledge to impress other Christians are not humble learners, either. Jesus said that making a display of our religious acts is just another form of pride (Matt. 6). It is not how much we have learned of God's Word in the *past* that makes us teachable, but how open we are to what God would show us *today.*

Jesus said, "Come to me . . . learn from me." Every Christian should have a continuing desire to know more of Christ. We can never feel as though we have already obtained all the insight we need or have already become mature (Phil. 3:10, 12).

We will miss much of what God has to teach us if we think He can speak only in special surroundings or through famous teachers. The Bible tells us to "let the word of Christ dwell . . . richly" in us so that we can teach and counsel one another with all wisdom (Col. 3:16). Those who have humble hearts will eagerly learn about the Lord from anyone who correctly handles the Word of Truth (2 Tim. 2:15). They will be judged to be "of more noble character" if they receive the message with great eagerness and examine the Scriptures every day to see if what their teachers say is true (Acts 17:11).

The Humble Are Obedient

Jesus said, "Come to me . . . take my yoke upon you . . . learn from me" (Matt. 11:28, 29). He also said, "If you love me, you will obey what I command" (John 14:15). It takes a much greater humility to obey someone than merely to listen to him. Yet can we be called teachable if we do not do what we are taught?

Christians are those who have come to Christ and who have said they love Him. Nevertheless it seems that many of us Christians have a great capacity for selective obedience. We are sometimes proud of our correct doctrine while allowing ourselves to behave in ways that doctrine forbids. We sometimes even choose the church we attend and the teachers we favor because they emphasize teachings we prefer and because they tread lightly on the areas that make us uncomfortable. We sometimes spend hours in Bible studies and church services, without their causing any change in us. We give the appearance of being teachable, but we are not obedient. Jesus said that those who hear His words but do not put them into practice are foolish (Matt. 7:26). James said, "Do not merely listen to the word, and so deceive yourselves. Do what it says" (1:22).

Too many Christians have their habits, actions, and speech under control but allow themselves to harbor desires, thoughts, and motives that do not honor Christ. Jesus said it is hypocritical when "people honor me with their lips, but their hearts are far from me" (Matt. 15:8), for the heart's disobedience is revealed in sinful behavior (Matt. 15:16–19).

Selective obedience is about as safe as playing Russian roulette. We may avoid disaster for a while, but eventually our hidden sins, unless removed, will pop out. We must be as diligent about the unseen as the seen and "take captive every thought to make it obedient to Christ" (2 Cor. 10:5) as we humble ourselves before God to do His will. Each of us will never know God's richest blessings as long as half of our heart is hardened. His greatest commandment is that we love Him with *all* our heart, soul, strength, and mind (Matt. 22:37). To obey only part of His commandment is hardly obedience at all.

The Humble Are Submissive

There is really little difference between being obedient and being submissive. Both mean to yield to the will or authority of another. But where obedience connotes action, submission perhaps refers more to attitude. It is possible to obey without being submissive in spirit, to do what we are told reluctantly and grudgingly.

The Bible says that we are to submit to one another as we teach each other through Scripture and song (Eph. 5:19–21). The Bible also says that wives are to submit to their husbands, and children are to obey and honor their parents (Eph. 5:22–24; 6:1–3). Submission is not a teeth-gritting, resentful response but a loving reverence for others.

Moses was called humble not because he lacked leadership qualities or intelligence, but because he submitted to God's authority. He served the people he was sent to lead rather than lording it over them.

The measure of our pride is often the level of struggle we encounter within ourselves over this command to submit.

The humble woman submits to those whom God has placed over her "out of reverence for Christ" (Eph. 5:21).

The Humble Are Gentle

Jesus said, "I am gentle and humble in heart . . ." (Matt. 11:29). One of our most precious images of our Lord is that of the shepherd tenderly carrying a lamb. Yet Christians often show a lack of true humility by the harsh way they respond to others who are also the Lord's sheep. Even His undershepherds are often not treated with respect. Paul had to appeal to the Corinthians by the meekness and gentleness of Christ to stop tearing him down in his absence. Yet in order "to live a life worthy of the calling you have received," we are told to "be completely humble and gentle; be patient, bearing with one another in love" (Eph. 4:1–2).

Women especially are called to gentleness. When we adopt the confrontational and aggressive tactics of the world, we are violating the nature God gave us. Paul said that when the apostles came to the Thessalonians "we were gentle among you, like a mother caring for her little children" (1 Thess. 2:7). Women should be an example of tenderness, not pride themselves on being as tough as any man. The Bible says that a woman's special grace should be "the unfading beauty of a gentle and quiet spirit, which is of great worth in God's sight. For this is the way the holy women of the past who put their hope in God used to make themselves beautiful" (1 Peter 3:4–5).

The Humble Are Prayerful

Prayer itself is an act of humility. It is an admission that we are not able to make our way on our own, that we need God. Even Christians, however, can tend to try to work things out on their own, praying only when they get into a "serious" situation. But the Bible says it is our pride that keeps us from seeking God (Ps. 10:4); the prouder we are, the less time we will spend in prayer. The Lord said that only when His people humbled themselves and prayed would He heal their land (2 Chron. 7:14).

Our resistance to prayer is evident when we compare attendance at prayer groups to attendance at Bible study groups. Prayer groups tend to die out much more quickly, and in the groups that do survive, the time of actual praying is often shorter than the time spent taking prayer requests.

The humble do not feel that prayer is a waste of time. For them it is the foundation of all godly action, a guard against the temptation to go off on their own, and a precious time of fellowship with their Lord God. It is also an activity that shows their obedience to His command:

> Seek the LORD, all you humble of the land, you who do what he commands. Seek righteousness, seek humility; perhaps you will be sheltered on the day of the LORD's anger.   Zephaniah 2:3

DIGGING DEEPER

1. What character traits, positive and negative, were discussed in this chapter? _____

_____

_____

2. How do you relate humility to the lessons from David in chapter 2? _____

_____

_____

3. What character traits are revealed in the following? What risk or cost is involved in each case?

   a. Mark 7:24–30 _____

_____

b. Mark 14:35−36 _____

_____

c. Luke 1:38 _____

_____

d. Luke 10:39 _____

_____

e. John 2:5−7 _____

_____

f. Acts 1:14 _____

_____

g. Acts 2:42 _____

_____

h. Acts 9:10−17 _____

_____

i. Philippians 2:3−4 _____

_____

4. In what ways do the following Scriptures say are we often proud? Relate your answers to the volcano illustration.
   a. Proverbs 18:12 _____
   b. Isaiah 10:12−13 _____
   c. Isaiah 23:9 _____
   d. Hosea 13:6 _____
   e. Luke 14:7−11 _____
   f. Luke 18:9−14 _____
   g. 1 Corinthians 1:11−12; 4:6 _____
   h. 2 Corinthians 5:12 _____
 5. Read Numbers 12.

a. How did Moses show his humility? _____

_____

b. What was the issue at stake? _____

_____

c. How could Moses have chosen to act? _____

_____

d. What can you learn from Miriam's and Aaron's actions? _____

_____

e. What can you learn from Moses' actions? _____

_____

6. What can you learn from Deuteronomy 8:2—5 about God's methods of teaching humility? _____

_____

_____

7. How did Saul practice selective obedience in 1 Samuel 15:1—26? What was the result? _____

_____

8. How important to your own welfare is your daily obedience to God's will (Deuteronomy 30:15—20)?_____

_____

_____

9. Does God think His requirements for obedience are too hard (Deuteronomy 30:11—14)?_____

_____

_____

10. Why do you think so many families are in trouble today? _____

_____

_____

11. In what areas of life are you being selectively obedient (or selectively disobedient) to God? _____

_____

_____

12. How does Romans 13:1–3 relate to the character traits discussed in this chapter? _____

_____

13. a. Why do you think women find it difficult to carry out the teaching in 1 Peter 3:1–6? _____

_____

b. If a married woman follows this teaching, what response from her husband can she ask God for? (v. 1) _____

_____

c. Why would this kind of behavior change some husbands' attitudes toward God? _____

_____

14. In what ways do you think women could be more gentle? _____

_____

_____

4

A CONTENTED HEART

Do not let your hearts be troubled. Trust in God; trust also in me (John 14:1).

Janice is plagued by persistent dissatisfaction with her life. She, her husband, and two children have lived in their present home for three years. Though she was excited about the house when they bought it, she now finds herself reading the housing ads in the newspaper. In fact, she reads the weekly classified section from end to end, thinking about all the things she would like to buy. She would like to talk to her husband about these items, but she knows it would only cause problems. Janice doesn't understand how everyone else seems to be able to give their children gymnastics, dancing, swimming, and music lessons, or where they find the money to go skiing on weekends and to keep buying the latest gadgets.

She enjoys her church activities and her children's sports events, but life seems dull. She has thought about taking a class of some kind, but would it be worth the effort? She thinks about getting a job so she will have the money to do some of the things she dreams about as she reads the newspaper ads.

Like millions of women today, Janice has a basic problem that she has not correctly identified. Because she does not recognize the real problem, she may make many wrong decisions as she tries to solve it.

Women's liberation groups do not tend to help women in their search for contentment, for contented women are seldom crusaders. Many of these organizations try to keep women feeling dissatisfied and agitated so the organization can obtain the woman's help in reaching its goals. The organizations add to the confusion by insisting that if discrimination and oppression are relieved women will be satisfied. They suggest that the answer to women's frustrations is material and monetary.

Using this same mentality, unhappy couples keep moving from house to house, from job to job, from community to community, hoping that the right environment will magically make everything rosy. Their moves statistically take them westward until they reach the Pacific coast, and even more recently, to Hawaii. When they cannot run any farther from their problems, divorce or suicide often become solutions.

The Bible, however, proclaims that the source of most of our dissatisfaction is not external but internal; that when we change houses, or life situations, or even marriage partners, we almost invariably take our unresolved troubles with us. Paul did not say, "I have found a way to change circumstances so they are more palatable to me." No, he said, "I have learned the secret of being content in any and every situation, whether well fed or hungry, whether living in plenty or in want" (Phil. 4:12). And then he told us what the secret is.

Do you want to know Paul's secret? Would you like to

learn how to be content? Here is the formula many people would pay millions for, and it is yours free: "I can do everything through him who gives me strength" (Phil. 4:13).

What a letdown! Here are the women of the world waiting for some startling method to make their circumstances more satisfying, and all they get are religious platitudes!

Contentment Equals Trust

But Paul is not spouting religious nonsense. What he is saying is that contentment equals trust. He is saying that the central questions the discontented of the world must answer are these: Is God in control of my life? Do I trust Him? Do I believe everything is for my best? If the answer is no, there is no hope for contentment. We may take up interesting hobbies, or we may get jobs and consequently have more money and less time to brood about our feelings of discontent. But we will remain just as empty and dissatisfied at the core of our existence, because we will not have dealt with the real issue. We have merely postponed facing it until the novelty of our activities wears off.

Paul, who endured all kinds of pain and hardship, said that changing circumstances will not bring contentment, because contentment is a matter of attitude, not situation. "If we have food and clothing, we will be content with that" (1 Tim. 6:8).

That doesn't mean, of course, that every time we experience restlessness we must immediately decide we have sinned. Life isn't that simple. Sometimes restlessness is God's call for us to make changes. And real change can be hard to make after we're securely settled and neatly defined. So we need to come before God and ask Him about the source of our discontent—is it our sinfulness and refusal to accept our lot in life; or is it His call to move out in some new direction. (This takes trust, too.)

God may call us into changed circumstances, but the level of contentment in our new situation is still a matter of attitude. Paul's life of experiencing both need and plenty taught him not to depend on externals for satisfaction. "If we have enough food and clothing," he says, "we will be content with that" (1 Tim. 6:8).

Envy Destroys Contentment

The crux of discontent often lies here: We find it hard indeed to be content with food and clothing. Janice's depression actually centered on comparing her lifestyle with others'.

> What causes fights and quarrels among you? Don't they come from your desires that battle within you? You want something but don't get it. You kill and covet, but you cannot have what you want. You quarrel and fight. You do not have, because you do not ask God. When you ask, you do not receive, because you ask with wrong motives, that you may spend what you get on your pleasures.   James 4:1–3

If we are truthful, we will admit that the most common cause of our discontent is our persistent desire for more material possessions. The advertising industry spends millions of dollars to keep us that way. Money is the number one cause of discord between husband and wife, and covetousness and envy harm more friendships than we probably realize. But God says the knowledge of His presence should raise the focus of our ambitions above the merely material, and that we can trust Him to take care of us. "Keep your lives free from the love of money and be content with what you have, because God has said, 'Never will I leave you; never will I forsake you' " (Heb. 13:5).

Worry Kills Contentment

One of the main ways we display lack of trust in God is through worry. All of us worry occasionally, but with some women it is an obsessive-compulsive behavior pattern that dominates their thought lives. Worriers may keep acquaintances from realizing what a large problem they have, but close friends and family are affected by their constant negative frame of mind.

The main term used in the Bible for worry is "fret," and we are repeatedly told not to fret. Jesus indicated that we have control over how much we worry. He said, "Do not *let* your hearts be troubled. Trust in God; trust also in me." (John 14:1, emphasis mine). To worry is to disobey our Lord; disobedience is sin.

Therefore, Christians should know how to break this habit, the terrible tyranny that worry holds over their lives. The solution is the same as for every tenacious sin: confess, repent. Agree with God that your continuous worry pattern is sin and shows a lack of trust. Tell Him that you realize your fears do not come from Him, for "perfect love drives out fear" (1 John 4:18). Then repent. That is, turn around from the direction you are going (in this case, the direction of your thoughts). By an act of your will, call on God to help you fill your mind with trusting, healthy, positive thoughts (Phil. 4:8).

Every time you start to worry, go through this process. Force your mind to dwell on the goodness of your life in God rather than on all the imaginings of a fearful heart. Slowly but surely you will break your debilitating habit.

Our worries usually center on the four possible losses we may suffer in life: loss of possessions, position, health, or loved ones. All of these are God's to give or take away, and all the worry in the world will not help us face these calmly, even if the things we imagine do happen. Worry will ruin the good days if we let it, while giving no solace in the difficult ones. Only God knows our future, and He wants us to leave fretting behind and trust Him with our possessions, our positions, our loved ones, our very lives.

Bitterness Poisons Contentment

Besides worry, perhaps the most prevalent negative character trait among Christian women is bitterness—a strong resentment over some incident or series of incidents in the past. Women seem to have a great capacity for storing up hurts, mulling them over, and working out exactly what they are going to say when the moment for retaliation comes.

We may tell ourselves that we can harbor such feelings and still be doing well spiritually, but others are not fooled. Bitterness is a character trait that is impossible to hide. Our negative ponderings are betrayed by our grim facial expressions, by our smiles that never quite reach the eyes. Without realizing it, our conversations have a nagging or sarcastic tone that reveal we are miserable. A woman filled with resentment is unpredictable, striking out verbally at others in anger, or making snide comments that catch innocent bystanders unaware, often hurting those who have no relation to the problem.

Peter said that those who are full of bitterness are captives to sin (Acts 8:23). They are also prisoners of the past. Often their thoughts are dominated by the person they feel mistreated them, even though he or she may be dead. Their sin is refusing to forgive the one who offended them and to trust God to use their painful pasts for their good. Their unforgiving spirit constitutes a ball and chain.

Jesus said to pray, "Forgive us our debts, as we also have forgiven our debtors" (Matt. 6:12). Sometimes we can talk ourselves into believing we have forgiven our offenders while still carrying resentment in our hearts. This is not true forgiveness. Real forgiveness expressed toward our oppres- sors frees us from our mental anguish, releases the hold on our thought processes, and restores our relationships with others. This is God's kind of forgiveness toward us, one that holds no grudges and forgets as well as forgives (Heb. 8:12).

One woman who really forgave her unfaithful husband said to me, "If anyone had told me how unimportant that period of my life would become to me, I would not have believed her. But it has." Only by truly ridding ourselves of bitterness can we keep from wounding others with the kinds of words and deeds that inevitably flow from bitter hearts.

Contented Heart, Grateful Heart

A person cannot be bitter, envious, or worried, and be grateful at the same moment. In each case we are concentrat- ing on what we are lacking in our lot in life rather than concentrating on our benefits. We can find aspects of any situation to displease us. We can be angry because a husband is out of work, or because he spends too much time on the job. We can worry about our own safety, or if nothing disturbs us personally, we can be on edge over tragic news from foreign countries. We can envy someone who has more freedom because they are childless, or someone who has more healthy children than we do. We can either latch on to the negative areas of our lives, or refuse to do so. To refuse the negative thoughts, we must center on all the things for which we can be grateful.

God says we should not only thank Him *in* every situation (1 Thess. 5:18), but also *for* everything (Eph. 5:20). I do not pretend to know how people can do that if, for example, a child dies, or a mate is unfaithful. But the Lord knows us best, and He says we need to find something for which to praise Him even in the darkest hours. Praise is not a flight from reality, but an attempt to see beyond the present moment to the reality of God's purpose for us and our loved ones.

Thankfulness is therapeutic. As long as we continue to wring our hands in anguish, those hands cannot help anyone. A mind in the turmoil of depression has little room for the recognition of God's presence and goodness. But if we focus our attention, through an act of the will, on the Lord Jesus Christ and His plan for us; if we force, if necessary, words of gratitude from our mouths; we will begin to find the contentment He gives and become useful to Him.

> Enter his gates with thanksgiving and his courts with praise; give thanks to him and praise his name. For the LORD is good and his love endures forever; his faithfulness continues through all generations. Psalm 100:4, 5

Contented Heart, Patient Heart

It is common to hear women bemoaning their lack of patience as if it were the most difficult gift to pry from God's hand. In fact, impatience stems almost solely from our exaggerated notions of what is due us. If we could but lower our estimation of the importance of *our* time, *our* plans, and *our* feelings, we would find ourselves almost automatically more patient.

If we are impatient about the same things that anger God—repeated sin, inattention to His Word, social injustice—we cannot really be called impatient (as long as our opinions are expressed in love). Neither can we expect a woman to remain totally unperturbed if someone smashes into her new car. Certainly "learning patience" is not an acceptable reason for failure to discipline a rebellious child. Patience is not the same thing as resignation or the cynical attitude that always expects the worst possible outcome.

Patience is a more positive trait. It is the ability to bear affliction, delay, and interruption with calmness, persever-ance, and confidence in the goodness of God (Col. 1:11, 12). It is inward peace as well as outward control. It is the submission of our schedules, our viewpoints, our dreams to the greater plan of God, with the conviction that He has a good reason for every delay He allows to come our way.

Contented Heart Authenticates Witness

A Christian leader tells of the time he was speaking to a church youth gathering and saw a group of rather tough-looking teenagers looking into the room from outside. He went out to invite the young people in to hear his presenta-tion. To his surprise, they were willing not only to talk to him, but also to give him their assessment of the Christians they recognized in the room. "That girl has peace, but that one doesn't," they informed him. "That boy has peace, but that one doesn't."

People form opinions about the worth of our faith as they watch us day by day. A contented woman exudes a quiet confidence that validates her verbal witness. A discontented woman is like a rumbling volcano who makes those around her uneasy and causes non-Christians to wonder what advantage there is in being a Christian.

This is not to say that the Lord does not use us even if we have problem areas in our lives. He can, and He does. We may let a bitterness fester, qualify as card-carrying worry-warts, complain constantly about lack of income, and He is still powerful enough to use us positively for Him. But this is no reason to allow our sin to go unchecked.

If we are not at peace about our lives, we must stop rebelling against the situations in which the Lord has placed us. We must ask Him to help us accept the situation in a way that will bring glory to Him, or to clearly reveal that our season of discontent is a call from Him to make a hard change. Then we will be more effective witnesses for Him. But even more important, then we will fulfill the Lord's desire for us: "Do not let your hearts be troubled. Trust in God; trust also in me" (John 14:1).

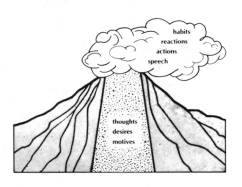

DIGGING DEEPER

1. What character traits, positive and negative, were discussed in this chapter? Do they relate to habits, reactions, actions, speech, desires, thoughts, or motives? _____

_____

_____

_____

2. How would you relate a contented heart to the humble heart discussed in chapter 3? _____

_____

_____

3. Look up the following Scripture to see about what and toward whom a person can be bitter.

a. Exodus 1:14 _____

b. Ruth 1:3−5, 11−13, 20 _____

c. 1 Samuel 1:10−15 _____

d. Psalm 73:3−13, 21 _____

e. Proverbs 17:25 _____

f. Ecclesiastes 7:26 _____

g. Jeremiah 2:19; 4:18 _____

h. Acts 8:18−23 _____

i. Colossians 3:21 _____

Do you need to confess bitterness in any of these areas?

_____

4. Read Genesis 3:1−6.

a. Was Eve's discontent caused by some lack in her circumstances? _____

b. How did Satan attack her contentment? _____

_____

_____

c. How does he use these same tactics on women today?

_____

_____

_____

5. Read Psalm 37:1−8.

a. What character trait are we warned against? _____

_____

b. Find at least four actions we can take to correct it. ____

_____

_____

6. Read Matthew 6:25–34.

a. What things does Jesus command us not to worry about? _____

_____

b. Why is worry futile? _____

_____

c. What does worry demonstrate? _____

_____

d. What positive action can we take to combat worry?

_____

7. a. How can individuals please God regarding their incomes (Luke 3:14; 1 Timothy 6:6–10; Hebrews 13:5)?

_____

_____

b. Do you think these passages mean it is a sin to seek a raise or to buy new things? _____

_____

_____

8. What is the difference between contentment and laziness (1 Thessalonians 4:11–12)? _____

_____

_____

9. If the Janice mentioned at the beginning of the chapter came to you for counsel, what would you say? _____

_____

_____

_____

10. In what circumstances did Paul show patience (2 Corinthians 6:3–10)? _____

_____

_____

11. Look up the following Scriptures to see in what other situations we are to express patience.

a. Proverbs 15:18 _____

b. Matthew 18:21–35 _____

c. 1 Thessalonians 5:14 _____

d. 2 Timothy 4:2 _____

e. James 5:7–11 _____

12. What can women learn about patience from the story of the Good Samaritan (Luke 10:30–35)? _____

_____

_____

13. What circumstances in your life are most difficult for you to be thankful for? _____

_____

_____

14. What benefits should we be grateful to God for (Psalm 103)? _____

_____

_____

_____

5

A FAITHFUL HEART

Be sure to fear the LORD and serve him faithfully with all your heart; consider what great things he has done for you (1 Sam. 12:24).

What is the greatest miracle? The divine healing of someone with a hopeless, terminal illness? A perfect new-born baby? Bringing a dead person back to life? The creation of the universe? Making a hardened criminal into a loving child of God?

For me, God's greatest miracle is a human life kept faithful to him for fifty years. Other miracles are often the work of an instant. But for someone to remain faithful through years of temptation, discouragement, and trial is a feat of such monumental proportions that one wonders that even God is up to the task.

People like to think that faithfulness is easy for a certain type of person . . . meaning, of course, someone other than themselves. But the failed marriages, misuse of church funds, and other problems of prominent Christians should make it obvious that no one is immune to the temptation to live on his or her own terms, and that "enduring to the end" does not happen automatically.

The Israelites were given one supernatural sign after another and were brought out of Egypt by miraculous means, but they still did not trust God enough to take the first opportunity He gave them to enter the Promised Land (Num. 13:30—14:10). King Saul knew what it was to experience personally the Holy Spirit's power in his life (1 Sam. 10:10; 11:6), but he ended up a deranged rebel. God gave Solomon "a wise and discerning heart, so that there will never have been anyone like you, nor will there ever be" (1 Kings 3:12), but in later life Solomon's heart turned away from the Lord, even to the extent of worshiping his foreign wives' gods! (1 Kings 11:7—10).

We cannot depend, then, on our past experiences of God's grace to keep us faithful in the present and future. In fact, those who have received much from God's hand sometimes seem more inclined to presume on His grace than gratefully to "consider what great things he has done for you" (1 Sam. 12:24).

Faithful Servants

Perhaps we would remain more faithful if we kept in mind our proper relationship to God. In the Bible, the word "faithful" is repeatedly linked with the words "serve" and "servant." If we consider ourselves God's servants, that very image should cause us to "fear the Lord" enough so that we take any disobedience seriously. When we forget we are to be humble servants, we begin to have heart trouble.

> So then, men ought to regard us as servants of Christ and as those entrusted with the secret things of God. Now it is required that those who have been given a trust must prove faithful. 1 Corinthians 4:1,2

Before we can be faithful servants, however, we must be sure we really *are* servants. A woman can walk into a restaurant kitchen and spend several days washing dishes, but when payday comes she will have no remuneration for her services if she was never actually hired. Someone might even grab a rifle and helmet and take part in the most grueling battle of a war without ever being a part of the army. Jesus said:

> Not everyone who says to me, "Lord, Lord," will enter the kingdom of heaven, but only he who does the will of my Father who is in heaven. Many will say to me on that day, "Lord, Lord, did we not prophesy in your name, and in your name drive out demons and perform many miracles?" Then I will tell them plainly, "I never knew you. Away from me, you evildoers!" Matthew 7:21–23.

Unfortunately, it is possible to serve *in the church* without being a servant *of the Lord*. But a person has to be hired by an employer to be an employee; must join the army to be a soldier; and must know Jesus Christ as personal Lord to be His servant. Otherwise, payday or retirement will come, and after many years of doing good deeds, the terrifying words will ring out, "I never knew you."

Becoming Jesus' servant is as definite an act as joining the army. We don't have to guess whether we've been inducted into the military or not . . . we are signed, sealed, and delivered. Neither do we have to be unsure about whether we have ever really become Christians. When we ask God to forgive us and make us one of His own, He sends the Holy Spirit to dwell in us as God's seal that we belong to Him (Eph. 1:13,14). It is the Holy Spirit within us that reassures us we are truly one of His children. If you have never "enlisted" in Christ's service, why not do so now? It will be impossible to be a faithful servant if you are not a servant at all.

Faithful Abraham

The Bible says that God found Abraham's heart faithful toward Him (Neh. 9:7, 8). This statement is not based on one spectacular act of devotion on Abraham's part (although his willingness to offer up his only son Isaac at God's command would certainly qualify). Rather, Abraham was a lifelong servant of God. As a young married man, he left his tribe behind at God's call, and with his wife, set out without any idea where God was leading him. He died at the age of 175, still obeying God by sending far away for a wife for his son so he would not intermarry with the surrounding pagans. Abraham was called faithful because he persevered. That is, he remained constant over the long haul, despite the obstacles (Heb. 11:8, 9).

Perseverance is an integral part of faithfulness. A spouse who is only faithful for a week, or a month, or a year, cannot be called faithful at all. Yet Christians have a tendency to feel that spurts of devotion or a few years of dependable service in some specific ministry discharge their commitment to the Lord. But God's commendation is given to a more tenacious kind of disciple.

> I know your deeds, your hard work and your perseverance. . . . You have persevered and have endured hardships for my name, and have not grown weary.
>
> Revelation 2:2, 3

The Faithful Endure

We hear about "endurance tests" for mechanical devices and even for the human body, and we admire automobiles and individuals that can take a lot of punishment. Few of us, however, seek these kinds of experiences for ourselves. But the Bible makes it clear that, seek them or not, all Christians will have endurance tests. We are not only expected to survive them, but also to do so joyously and victoriously (James 1:2–4).

Endurance in the Christian life conjures up an image of one so beset by persecution and pain that the issue is survival rather than progress. We are aware that believers through the centuries have suffered and died because of their faith, and that there are those suffering right now in Communist countries. But such trials seem remote and unreal to most Christians in Western countries. We are a pampered lot, sometimes caving in at even the first sign of opposition.

God says, "Be faithful, even to the point of death . . ." (Rev. 2:10). All too often, however, our courage fails in the face of simply a harsh word, an embarrassed silence, or a cooled relationship. Any time our beliefs clash with those of others around us, we are tempted to become unfaithful rather than endure a slight. But God's way leads through the valley of the shadow of death, and He will allow repeated trials to come into our lives so that we ". . . may be mature and complete, not lacking anything" (James 1:4). If we fail the tests, we will remain immature, incomplete, unfaithful, and will probably find ourselves facing similar tests over and over until we pass . . . or until we entirely quench the Spirit's efforts to teach us.

Part of our problem with enduring stems from our expectation of a prosperous and protected life as part of God's "forever family." We overlook the warnings in Scripture and concentrate on the happy messages and promises we find there. But Peter tells us clearly that we are foolish to be caught offguard by adversity:

> Dear friends, do not be surprised at the painful trial you are suffering, as though something strange were happening to you. But rejoice that you participate in sufferings of Christ. . . .   1 Peter 4:12,13

And Paul gets very specific when he writes:

> To this very hour we go hungry and thirsty, we are in rags, we are brutally treated, we are homeless. We work hard with our own hands. When we are cursed, we bless; when we are persecuted, we endure it; when we are slandered, we answer kindly. Up to this moment we have become the scum of the earth, the refuse of the world.
> 1 Corinthians 4:11–13

The suffering that God calls us to endure faithfully is not identical for every believer. But whether our trials come in the form of physical pain, economic deprivation, emotional suffering, or actual threat of life, God provides us with the means to remain faithful.

> We do not want you to be uninformed, brothers, about the hardships we suffered in the province of Asia. We were under great pressure, far beyond our ability to endure, so that we despaired even of life. Indeed, in our hearts we felt the sentence of death. But this happened that we might not rely on ourselves but on God, who raises the dead. He has delivered us from such a deadly peril, and he will deliver us. On him we have set our hope that he will continue to deliver us. . . .
> 2 Corinthians 1:8–10

The Faithful Are Steadfast

One of the keys to enduring and persevering is to be absolutely convinced that we are right. If we have doubts about our beliefs, we will be "like a wave of the sea, blown and tossed by the wind," like "a double-minded man, unstable in all he does" (James 1:6,8).

In contrast, the steadfast woman stands firm on the basis of what Scripture teaches and is not confused by people who would like to "worm their way into homes and gain control over weak-willed women," women who are ". . . always learning but never able to acknowledge the truth" (2 Tim. 3:6, 7). To be steadfast is to be fixed firmly in place, unchanging, immovable.

We need to be steadfast not only in our Christian commitment, but also in our personal relationships. Our husbands, our children, our friends should be able to depend on us to be there when it counts. They should never have to worry about their standing with us or our commitment to them. Our steadfast faithfulness to our husbands causes us to avoid even the first step toward intimacy with another man. The steadfast woman experiences a clear conscience and a unity of purpose that gives her life an aura of tranquility unknown to the unstable.

> You will keep in perfect peace him whose mind is steadfast, because he trusts in you.   Isaiah 26:3

The Faithful Are Loyal

David is perhaps the most striking example of loyalty in the Bible. Despite Saul's relentless hounding and continual attempts to kill him, David's repeated response was, "But the LORD forbid that I should lay a hand on the LORD's anointed" (1 Sam. 26:11). Even as Saul searched for David, it was said, "Who of all your servants is as loyal as David?" (1 Sam. 22:14).

It is possible to be faithful without being loyal. A woman could be pure in her thoughts and actions, never even looking at another man, without exhibiting real loyalty toward her husband. Loyalty is not merely the absence of disloyalty, but an active promotion of the other person's welfare. A woman who is loyal to her husband, children, and friends speaks well of them, brings their good qualities to light, and endeavors to show her appreciation of them in every way possible. She defends them against undue criticism and tries tactfully to help them change less desirable characteristics. "Her husband has full confidence in her" because "... she brings him good, not harm, all the days of her life" (Prov. 31:11,12).

Loyalty to God is also active, a "jealousy for His name" that causes us to speak up for Him rather than be silent. Loyalty to God includes loyalty to other believers, and living a life that will bring honor to the Lord rather than hold Him up to ridicule.

> O LORD, God of our fathers Abraham, Isaac and Israel, keep this desire in the hearts of your people forever, and keep their hearts loyal to you.   1 Chronicles 29:18

The Faithful Are Trustworthy

Having an untrustworthy servant can be worse than having no servant at all. Think of the harm one dishonest steward could cause his master. Think of the harm God's servants cause when they are not trustworthy.

Being trustworthy encompasses such basic character traits as honesty, dependability, truthfulness, and sincerity. And though these qualities are taught from the cradle on up, Christians seem to struggle with them as much as anyone. We need to be reminded that God detests anyone who deals dishonestly (Deut. 25:16).

Perhaps our biggest problem is that we allow ourselves small hypocrisies or white lies without remembering that sin is contagious, sin spreads, and sin compounds. If we think that bringing home unauthorized supplies from work, or eating some grapes at a market before we pay for them, or leaving a task unfinished is a minor thing, we should hear again Jesus' words:

> Whoever can be trusted with very little can also be trusted with much, and whoever is dishonest with very little will also be dishonest with much. So if you have not been trustworthy in handling worldly wealth, who will trust you with true riches? Luke 16:10–11

God Is Faithful

One of the most tremendous things about God is that "if we are faithless, he will remain faithful, for he cannot disown himself" (2 Tim. 2:13). He endures our disobedience and perseveres in His graciousness toward us: "He is faithful and just and will forgive us our sins and purify us from all unrighteousness" (1 John 1:9). The miracle of God's forgiveness can be part of an even greater miracle in your life—the miracle of lifelong faithfulness, faithfulness even to the point of death. Then you can look forward to hearing Him say, "Well done, good and faithful servant!" (Matt. 25:21).

DIGGING DEEPER

1. What character traits were included in this chapter? ____

_____

_____

_____

2. Read Hebrews 11:8–19.

a. List the ways in which Abraham showed his faithfulness. _____

_____

_____

_____

_____

_____

b. What could God ask of you that would be equal in each instance to what God required of Abraham? _____

_____

_____

_____

_____

_____

3. Read Hebrews 11:32−38.

a. What kinds of things have God's people been asked to endure? _____

_____

_____

_____

b. What "endurance tests" has God given you in your lifetime? How faithful have you been? _____

_____

_____

_____

4. What is the purpose of the trials of life, according to the following Scripture?

a. Romans 5:3−4 _____

_____

b. 2 Corinthians 1:8–10 _____

_____

c. Hebrews 5:8; 12:7–12 _____

_____

d. James 1:2–4 _____

_____

5. In what other areas of life should we be faithful?

a. Malachi 2:15–16 _____

_____

b. Romans 12:12 _____

_____

c. 1 Peter 4:10 _____

_____

d. 3 John, verses 1–5 _____

_____

Assign one or more of the following to the above: habit, action, reaction, speech, desire, thought, motive.

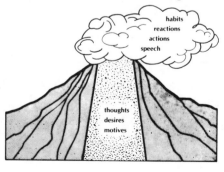

6. Read Matthew 25:14–30.

a. What does the master expect from his faithful servants? _____

_____

_____

b. How would you apply this to today? What does God expect from us who believe? _____

_____

c. How does God feel about unproductive Christians?

_____

d. What motivated the third servant in this story? How did the master react to this view? _____

_____

e. Do you think there is a biblical basis for this kind of motivation? What Scriptures would you cite? _____

_____

f. What other motivations can servants have? _____

_____

g. How did the master in the parable reward his faithful servants (see especially vv. 21, 23)? _____

_____

h. When do you think God expects His servants to retire from active duty? Why do you think this? _____

_____

_____

i. What do you think Christians mean when they say they are "burned out" in the service of the Lord? What would you say to such a person? _____

_____

_____

_____

j. According to this Scripture, if a person is never entrusted with large tasks by God, what could be the reason?

_____

k. What do you think is a "large" task in God's eyes? ___

_____

_____

7. What kind of people did Paul want as co-workers (1 Corinthians 4:17; Ephesians 6:21; Colossians 1:7; 4:7; 4:9. Compare with 2 Timothy 4:9, 10)? _____

_____

_____

What kind of a co-worker are you (see Proverbs 25:19)?

_____

8. Relate the parable in Luke 8:5–15 to the character traits in this chapter in as many ways as you can. _____

_____

_____

_____

9. In Luke 17:5, Jesus' disciples ask for more faith. In response, the Lord tells a parable about a servant. Read Luke 17:5–10 and answer the following:

a. How does being faithful differ from being full of faith?

_____

_____

_____

b. How does Jesus' parable relate to the disciples' question? _____

_____

_____

c. How does the parable affect your concept of a faithful servant? _____

_____

_____

d. What light does this passage shed on the importance of spectacular evidences of faith (verse 6)? _____

_____

_____

10. In what areas of life is it most difficult for you to be faithful? _____

_____

_____

_____

_____

11. What changes are you willing to make to please the Lord? _____

_____

_____

_____

6

A DILIGENT HEART

Watch over your heart with all diligence, for from it flow the springs of life (Prov. 4:23, NASB).

In 1831, Dr. John Snow single-handedly stemmed the London cholera epidemic. Through painstaking detection, he isolated the cause of the infection to a single water pump, which was then shut down.

In 1981, an alert bank employee spotted irregularities in some computer entries and triggered an investigation that uncovered what federal prosecutors called the nation's largest bank swindle. A bank manager, a bank employee, and a boxing promoter were convicted on more than thirty counts of transporting stolen property, embezzlement, and conspiracy.

Such examples of the results of diligence are inspiring, but unfortunately rare. Diligence—persistent, attentive, and energetic application to a task—is not a prominent character trait in our society. Employees seldom express fervent loyalty for their employers or display much zeal in tackling the tasks assigned to them. People tend to want positions rather than jobs, viewing work as an intrusion in their lives rather than a vocation. As a result, it is far easier to cite instances where harm resulted from indifference and sloth than occasions when careful attention saved the day.

Differing Personalities

Some people have a natural aptitude for handling details, an inherent industriousness that makes diligence easy for them. They are born organizers and cannot rest until everything on their list—and they love lists—is crossed off for the day. Others of us are more casual, moving from one worthwhile activity to another without worrying about the order in which they are completed—and sometimes not even worrying about if they all get done.

But in the Bible God commands us all to be diligent, as well as faithful and humble. If one attribute comes more easily to us, we should be grateful. But we are not excused from the necessity of gaining a particular character trait simply because it does not come to us naturally.

On the other hand, it is possible to think mistakenly that we are displaying godly character traits when we are actually doing the opposite. People with neurotic or obsessive-compulsive tendencies can appear diligent when in fact they are acting out of fear and anxiety rather than a desire to please God. Such people seem at first to be wonderful additions to a church, but they soon cause problems because of their rigidity and their need to be in control. They seldom experience the joy of service because no amount of attention to detail assuages their anxieties about possible failure. Their lack of flexibility and their possessive attitudes kill the joy in others as well.

The obsessive-compulsive woman also has problems at home. She is organized, not from a desire to do the right thing, but from fear of what will happen if anything should slip from her control. She does not trust God to take care of her; she must see to everything herself. She invites company to dinner but makes her family miserable preparing for the company. Then she keeps the guests uneasy because she is constantly hopping around organizing them instead of spending time enjoying them.

In Luke 10:40—41 we are told that on one occasion, when Martha and Mary were entertaining Jesus in their home, Martha "was distracted by all the preparations that had to be made." She complained, "Lord, don't you care that my sister has left me to do the work by myself? Tell her to help me!" Jesus' replied that Martha was "worried and upset about many things." His response should cause us to review our own attitudes as we serve the Lord. Our "diligence" may really be anxiety and a need to control events that makes life difficult for ourselves and others.

Diligence in Temporal Matters

Different versions of the Bible may use words other than "diligent," such as "watchful," "alert," "pay close attention," "beware," "guard," "take pains," "be absorbed," or "be careful." The opposing concept may be indicated by the words "slothful," "sluggard," "lazy," or "neglectful." But whatever phrase is used, the clear teaching is that God expects His people to be industrious in their daily work.

> Diligent hands will rule, but laziness ends in slave labor. . . . The sluggard craves and gets nothing, but the desires of the diligent are fully satisfied.
>
> Proverbs 12:24; 13:4

> Make it your ambition to lead a quiet life, to mind your own business and to work with your hands, just as we told you, so that your daily life may win the respect of

outsiders and so that you will not be dependent on
anybody.   1 Thessalonians 4:11−12

Train the younger women to love their husbands and
children, to be self-controlled and pure, to be busy at
home, . . . so that no one will malign the word of God.
                                                    Titus 2:4,5

Our desire to please God is revealed by how well we do
our routine work. Earthly masters are to be served "not only
when their eye is on you and to win their favor, but with
sincerity of heart and reverence for the Lord. Whatever you
do, work at it with all your heart, as working for the Lord, not
for men" (Col. 3:22−23). What has derisively been called
the Puritan work ethic is obviously not the narrow-minded
view of a religious sect, but a command from God's Word
that includes the promise of reward for obedience (Col.
3:23−24).

If we are diligent in our everyday affairs, we will also be
prompt. We will write down our commitments and be sure to
get to them on time. Our alertness will include watching the
clock, not to make sure we don't work an extra minute, but
to allow ourselves enough time to get to our appointments.

Some people have a habit of tardiness. This is sometimes
caused by laziness or by rebellion. It may stem from a desire
to have others wait on them or a perhaps unconscious
resolve not to let anyone tell them what to do or when to do
it. The diligent person is more likely to try to be early than
choose to be late, for she cannot be carrying out her tasks
with careful attention if she is not even there.

Diligence in Spiritual Matters

But as our key verse at the beginning of the chapter
indicates, the Bible has even more to say about the necessity
of diligence in spiritual matters than in temporal ones. We

must watch over our hearts carefully because, as we learned in the first chapter, they are "deceitful above all else" and prone to spiritual sicknesses of all kinds. If, as Jesus said, evil thoughts, sexual immorality, theft, murder, adultery, greed, malice, deceit, lewdness, envy, slander, arrogance, and folly can all come from our hearts and make us unclean (Mark 7:20–23), we must constantly guard our hearts' spiritual condition. Otherwise, the "springs of life" that should flow from our hearts will become springs of death.

In almost every war movie I have ever seen, invaders have breached supposedly impregnable fortresses because the patrolling soldiers have, through overconfidence or laxity, let down their guard. Our souls have enemies, too, and one in particular prowls like a roaring lion hoping to devour us (1 Peter 5:8). Only watchfulness of the most assiduous kind will keep such an enemy at bay. Sporadic diligence will fail. Jesus' two-pronged defense is as necessary for us as it was for the disciples: "Watch and pray so that you will not fall into temptation. The spirit is willing, but the body is weak" (Matt. 26:41).

Christians are repeatedly told to be on their guard. We are warned against individuals who oppose the gospel (Matt. 10:16–17), against erroneous teaching (Rom. 16:17–18), and against false prophets (Matt. 7:15). We are to guard against our own greed (Luke 12:15), dissipation, drunkenness, the anxieties of life (Luke 21:34), and spiritual hypocrisy (Mark 12:38–40). The threats to our spiritual lives are from without and from within.

God Is Diligent

When we consider the spiritual warfare in which we are engaged and assess our chances of survival on our own, our hearts overflow with gratitude, for God does indeed watch over His children and protect us moment by moment. Our best efforts at spiritual diligence will not be good enough. But we can rest secure in the knowledge that the maker of heaven and earth is eternally vigilant.

> He will not let your foot slip—he who watches over you will not slumber; indeed, he who watches over Israel will neither slumber nor sleep. The LORD watches over you—the LORD is your shade at your right hand; the sun will not harm you by day, nor the moon by night. The LORD will keep you from all harm—he will watch over your life; the LORD will watch over your coming and going both now and forevermore. Psalm 121:3−8

DIGGING DEEPER

1. How would you relate diligence to faithfulness as it was discussed in the previous chapter? _____

_____

2. List some examples illustrating how one person's diligence can mean life or death for others. _____

_____

_____

3. Find at least fifteen words or phrases in this chapter that help define "diligence." Which of these terms could also be considered separate character traits? _____

_____

_____

_____

4. According to the following passages, in what areas of life are we to be diligent?

a. Deuteronomy 6:6–7 _____

_____

b. Deuteronomy 6:17 _____

_____

c. 2 Chronicles 24:13 _____

_____

d. Proverbs 21:5 _____

_____

e. Proverbs 31:27 _____

_____

f. Mark 13:32–37 _____

_____

g. Romans 16:17–18 _____

_____

h. Galatians 6:1 _____

_____

i. Ephesians 4:3 _____

_____

j. Ephesians 6:18 _____

_____

k. 1 Peter 5:8 _____

_____

Assign one of the following to each of the above: motive, desire, thought, speech, action, reaction, habit.

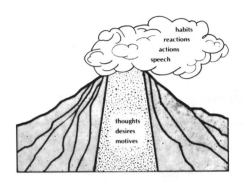

5. According to the following passages, what parts of the body are involved in diligence?

a. Psalm 141:3 _____

b. Proverbs 10:4; 12:24; 31:13, 19, 20 _____

c. Proverbs 4:25; 31:27; Hebrews 12:2 _____

d. Proverbs 31:17 _____

e. Proverbs 31:26; James 1:26 _____

f. Proverbs 1:15; Ecclesiastes 5:1 _____

g. Matthew 22:37; 2 Corinthians 10:5 _____

6. What effect would alcoholic beverages or drugs have on the exercising of the character traits discussed in this chapter, especially in relation to your answers to question 5? _____

_____

_____

_____

7. What should we learn from the ant (Proverbs 6:6−11)?

_____

_____

_____

_____

8. According to the following passages, when is promptness especially important?

    a. Leviticus 19:13; James 5:4 _____

    b. Deuteronomy 23:21; Ecclesiastes 5:4 _____

    c. Psalm 119:60 _____

    d. Matthew 5:23−24 _____

    e. Matthew 5:25−26 _____

    f. Ephesians 4:26 _____

    g. James 1:19 _____

9. a. List at least seven areas in which Timothy was exhorted to be a diligent pastor (1 Timothy 4:12−16). _____

_____

_____

_____

    b. What does this passage say will result from a pastor's diligence in these areas? _____

_____

    c. How does the list compare with your ideas about the priorities a pastor should have? _____

_____

10. Rewrite Proverbs 31:10–31 in your own words to reflect a modern version of the kind of wife Scripture commends. _____

_____

_____

_____

_____

_____

_____

_____

_____

_____

_____

_____

_____

_____

_____

_____

_____

_____

_____

_____

_____

What would you need to change to be an "excellent wife"? _____

_____

_____

11. a. List specific areas in which you need to be more diligent. _____

_____

_____

b. Write the names of the people who would be affected by changes in these areas and how your action would affect them. _____

_____

_____

_____

c. Begin now to be more diligent in prayer (Matthew 26:41) by spending time praying about these changes.

7

A COMPASSIONATE HEART

And so, as those who have been chosen of God, holy and beloved, put on a heart of compassion, kindness, humility, gentleness and patience; bearing with one another, and forgiving each other, whoever has a complaint against any one; just as the Lord forgave you, so also should you (Col. 3:12–13, NASB).

Of all the character traits in our study, the compassionate heart perhaps reflects most closely God's own heart. When Moses was given the Law on Mt. Sinai, the Lord chose to reveal His compassionate nature at this pivotal point in history:

> Then the LORD came down in the cloud and stood there with him and proclaimed his name, the LORD. And he passed in front of Moses, proclaiming, "The LORD, the LORD, the compassionate and gracious God, slow to anger, abounding in love and faithfulness, maintaining love to thousands, and forgiving wickedness, rebellion and sin. Yet he does not leave the guilty unpunished; he punishes the children and their children for the sin of the fathers to the third and fourth generation."
>
> Exodus 34:5–7

At the same time that He was proclaiming His standards for His people's conduct and the cost of disobedience, God longed for His chosen people to comprehend something of His love, forgiveness, mercy, and grace. God had previously revealed Himself through the awesome miracles of disaster and death that had accompanied their release from Egypt, and through the thunder, lightning, trumpet blast, earthquake, smoke, and fire that caused the people to tremble around Mt. Sinai (Exod. 19:16–18). But he also wanted His children to understand that He was slow to anger and compassionate toward them.

Compassion Focuses on Others

Compassion seems to reflect the essence of God's heart because it focuses on others rather than self. Unfortunately, it is possible for a woman to be diligent and self-centered at the same time. She can be loyal and steadfast without reaching out beyond those in her own little circle. She can be content and seem humble while remaining largely self-absorbed. But she cannot be compassionate without setting aside her own plans and comfort to meet the needs of others.

Jesus, in the ultimate expression of compassion, laid aside the glory that was His natural existence and "made himself nothing, taking the very nature of a servant, being made in human likeness. And being found in appearance as a man, he humbled himself and became obedient to death—even death on a cross!" (Phil. 2:7, 8).

In the same way, every act of kindness, every generous, sensitive, merciful word or deed on our part demands that we look beyond ourselves and our needs. It requires that we expend some effort for the sake of others in a way that reflects the nature of our self-giving Lord.

Compassion Is Active

Christians are sometimes accused of being so heavenly-minded that they are no earthly good. We get caught up in choir rehearsals, studies of the end times, or other church activities, and ignore needs around us. When problems are brought to our attention, we content ourselves with feeling sorry about them while doing nothing. But sympathetic thoughts or kindly musings are not true compassion.

With the divine power He possessed, Jesus could have met the multitudes' needs merely by forming a thought or speaking a command. He could even have done it from heaven without coming to earth. But His compassion caused Him not only to come and live and die among us, but also to touch lepers (Mark 1:40–41) and blind men (Matt. 20:34), and to take little children in His arms (Mark 10:13–16). It prompted Him to postpone plans for a much-needed respite from the demands of ministry to teach and feed the multitudes (Mark 6:31–34). True compassion is not passive wishful thinking or the donation of unwanted items to a worthy cause. It is personal, active involvement that expresses God's merciful heart in words and deeds.

There is a disturbing tendency on the part of some Christians to float around from church to church, sampling the best from each situation without committing themselves to any one fellowship. Perhaps one of the reasons they do this is because they realize that joining a church will require responsibility toward its members, and they prefer to remain unencumbered. When we serve with others, we have to learn to be gracious and to forgive each other when we offend or differ in opinions. When we are part of a particular body, we may be expected to help when others are sick or out of work, taking them meals or cleaning their houses, or caring for their children. It is awkward to refuse to help if we are church members. But if we choose instead to be perpetual visitors (to the largest churches possible, to assure anonymity), we are safe from such demands. We are at the same time losing opportunities to learn the character traits that are closest to God's heart.

Generosity, forgiveness, comfort, and forbearance can only be expressed in relationships, not in isolation. They must also be exhibited to all human beings, not just other believers. But if we shy away from involvement with brothers and sisters in Christ, it is unlikely that we will have much interest in the broken marriages, family problems, or physical needs of neighbors, much less those who are needy around the world.

Erupting with Compassion

We have said that the heart can be compared to a volcano, and we have noted Jesus' list of the foul things that can come out of our hearts, making us and those around us unclean. How wonderful it would be if instead of spewing out malice, envy, immorality, and deceit, our lives would erupt with veritable floods of forgiveness, graciousness, gentleness, and sympathy. What a blessing it would be if kindness, comfort, generosity, and mercy would flow from our lives to heal others, whether they be our own families or the destitute in far-off lands.

For more than one hundred years, Christians have formed the front line of a crusade to alleviate human suffering around the world. They have traveled the globe, building hospitals and bringing food and clothing even to peoples whose own political leaders cared nothing for their suffering. In slums and desolate places of our own country, God's servants have labored to bring health, hope, and salvation to the poor.

But we have also had to recall missionaries because the

funds to support them have dried up. Sometimes needs cannot be met because qualified people—carpenters, teachers, agriculturalists, health experts, secretaries—do not answer God's call to serve. Many Christians have become so dependent on their luxuries, so committed to the pursuit of the good life, that they have abdicated their roles as angels of mercy.

God's chosen people are to "put on a heart of compassion." We are to meet others' needs, not to continually satisfy our selfish desires. As God showers us with comfort through His Word and through other believers, we in turn are to redirect the stream of His mercy to others. We are not to hoard God's love, but to overflow with the good news of His compassion to all.

> Praise be to the God and Father of our Lord Jesus Christ, the Father of compassion and the God of all comfort, who comforts us in all our troubles, so that we can comfort those in any trouble with the comfort we ourselves have received from God.   2 Corinthians 1:3

DIGGING DEEPER

1. List at least eight character traits discussed in this chapter. _____

_____

_____

_____

What negative character traits would be the opposite of these? _____

_____

_____

2. a. What human conditions caused Jesus to feel compassion? (See Matthew 9:36; 14:14; 15:32; 20:34; Mark 1:40–41.) _____

_____

_____

_____

_____

b. What did Jesus' compassion cause Him to do in each case? _____

_____

_____

_____

c. For which people in your sphere of life would Jesus feel compassion? _____

_____

d. What would He have you do for them in His name?

_____

_____

3. a. How does the parable in Matthew 25:31–46 apply to the character traits in this chapter? _____

_____

_____

b. What is to be our motive for action? _____

_____

_____

c. Is the parable intended to show that our salvation depends on our works of compassion? (Use Matthew 25:34; John 3:16; Galatians 3:1–3; and James 2:14–18 to help form your answer.) _____

_____

_____

_____

4. Does God's compassion mean there is no punishment for sin? (See Exodus 34:4–7; Hebrews 12:5–11.) _____

_____

How should Christians express this dual nature of God in their attitudes and actions? _____

_____

_____

_____

5. How are we to show compassion in our business dealings?

    a. Exodus 22:26–27 _____

_____

    b. Deuteronomy 24:17–22 _____

_____

    c. Proverbs 22:7, 22 _____

_____

    d. Amos 5:11–12 _____

_____

e. Colossians 4:1 _____

_____

f. James 5:1–4 _____

_____

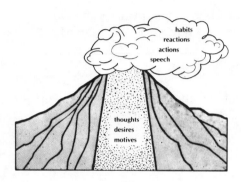

6. Read Luke 6:27–36. List in two columns the conduct of the godly and the contrasting conduct of the ungodly. Then assign one or more of the following to each: motive, desire, thought, speech, action, reaction, habit.

Conduct of the godly   *Conduct of the ungodly*

Conduct of the godly   *Conduct of the ungodly*

7. a. What character trait does the busy Christian woman especially need to remember (Romans 12:13; Hebrews 13:2; 1 Peter 4:9)? _____

_____

b. What is the difference between hospitality and entertaining (Romans 12:13)? _____

_____

c. How can we express hospitality in public situations (James 2:1−9)? _____

_____

d. What was the basis of Jesus' hospitality (Matthew 9:11−13; Luke 14:12−14)? _____

_____

e. How can a single woman show hospitality? A working mother? A shut-in? _____

_____

_____

_____

f. To whom are we not to show hospitality (1 Corinthians 5:9−13; 2 Timothy 3:1−7)? _____

_____

8. What is the mark of a gracious person (Proverbs 25:11; Luke 4:22; Colossians 4:6)? _____

_____

9. What specific instructions and cautions do we have to help us know what constitutes graciousness in speech?

    a. Psalm 12:2–4 _____

_____

    b. Psalm 141:3 _____

_____

    c. Ephesians 4:15 _____

_____

    d. Ephesians 5:4 _____

_____

    e. Ephesians 5:11–12 _____

_____

    f. 1 Timothy 5:13 _____

_____

    g. 1 Timothy 6:3,4 _____

_____

    h. 2 Timothy 2:16 _____

_____

    i. James 1:19 _____

_____

    j. 1 Peter 3:15 _____

_____

10. What does the Bible indicate is one purpose of wealth (Proverbs 22:9; Ephesians 4:28)? _____

_____

What instructions and cautions does God give to those who have more than they need? (See Luke 12:16–21; 2 Corinthians 9:6–12; 1 Timothy 6:17–19.) _____

_____

_____

_____

_____

11. What is often the cry of those in distress (Psalm 69:20)?

_____

12. a. What can we learn from Job's friends in Job 2:11–13 about showing sympathy? _____

_____

b. Can you illustrate the effect of similar conduct from an experience in your own life? _____

_____

13. How can we help those in distress?

a. Luke 3:11 _____

_____

b. Romans 15:1 _____

_____

c. Hebrews 10:32, 34 _____

_____

d. 1 Peter 3:8 _____

_____

14. What did Jesus mean when He quoted the Old Testament saying, "I desire mercy, not sacrifice" (Matthew 9:13; 12:7)? (See Amos 5:11–12, 21–24; Luke 11:42; 20:46–47.) _____

_____

_____

What do Christians today substitute for mercy? _____

_____

_____

_____

15. In what areas would the Lord want you to be more compassionate? _____

_____

_____

8

A CHEERFUL HEART

A cheerful heart is good medicine, but a crushed spirit dries up the bones (Prov. 17:22).

A man recently said to me, "There are two or three people in my life that I love to see coming, because they always lift my spirits." A few days before, a woman had said of an acquaintance, "Her smile lights up the whole room." That's the way it is, isn't it? Other people can raise our hopes or dash our spirits, improve our day, or all but ruin it.

Doctors tell us that a cheerful heart is indeed good medicine, and that people's attitudes toward life affect their health, and in some cases even determine whether they live or die. People with a more optimistic, positive approach to life have fewer physical ailments than do those with a hopeless, negative frame of mind.

Since both our health and our enjoyment of life are at stake, we Christians should pay special attention to the attitudes we are fostering. An anxious heart weighs us down (Prov. 12:25), causing us to miss much of the joy God desires for us and reflecting poorly on the One we are supposed to glorify.

Transcending Circumstances

I once heard a conference speaker tell of the time he asked one of his parishioners how she was doing, and she replied, "Pretty well, under the circumstances." He asked, "What in the world are you doing under there?" Rather than letting situations determine our emotional state, we are to transcend our circumstances, even to "give thanks in all circumstances, for this is God's will for you in Christ Jesus" (1 Thess. 5:18).

If our moods totally depend on the way life is going at any given moment, we are in a precarious position indeed. For life holds few perfect days, hours, or minutes. Every silver lining has a cloud. Every half full cup is also half empty.

Paul says he *learned* to be content in every circumstance (Phil. 4:12). This means that we can change and train ourselves to adopt a more cheerful attitude toward life. We can, through a desire to please God, choose to be joyful as an act of the will, refusing to be overwhelmed emotionally when things do not turn out as we want.

The Heart Defined

We have discussed various kinds of hearts in this study without defining the term as it is used in the Bible. The word translated "heart" in modern versions was occasionally translated as "reins" (kidneys) or "bowels" in the King James Version. Each of these terms is an attempt to signify the inner core of a person. The heart is the part of a person that thinks, feels, decides. It is a person's mind, emotions, and will.

We accept the mystery of God's Triune personality— Father, Son, Holy Spirit—without realizing that our make-up is also something of a mystery. We think of our spirits as that part of us that lives on after death. But that which expresses our personalities—our hearts (mind, emotions, will)—lives on too, giving our spirits our unique identities. Our physical bodies stay earthbound at death, yet during our lifetime our temporal bodies are the sole vehicles for communicating to others the thoughts, feelings, and decisions of our eternal hearts. At the same time, our emotions and our attitudes can affect the body that houses them, as we mentioned in the opening paragraphs of this lesson.

In addition, as Paul indicates, one part of the heart can rule over another part. The mind can instruct the will; the will can overrule the mind; the emotions can short-circuit every cautioning thought or holy intention. One part of the heart can even deceive another part, telling it that its motives are pure, when in fact it is rationalizing sin (Jer. 17:9).

It is no wonder that the Bible has so much to say about the heart and that Jesus warns us so strongly about heart trouble (Mark 7:21–23). We can see clearly why we are told to guard the heart as the wellspring of life (Prov. 4:23). As with a volatile chemical that needs to be kept at a carefully controlled temperature, the heart needs to be watched continuously.

Temperament and the Cheerful Heart

As with diligence, a woman's cheerfulness is closely linked to her personality type. To some people a sunny disposition just seems to come naturally, while others are serious or moody. Each type of temperament needs a word of caution.

Happy, bubbly women need to be sincere and not superficial in their personal relationships. They should not use their cheerfulness to avoid facing life's problems realistically. People around us are hurting. And while we cannot allow them to drag us down into the "slough of despond," neither should we pin clownlike smiles on our faces and ignore the reality of their pain. Proverbs 25:20 says that "one who sings songs to a heavy heart" is like "one who takes away a garment on a cold day, or like vinegar poured on soda." Christians must be sensitive to those times when a sympathetic ear is needed. To say, "Cheer up! Life is terrific!" to someone caught in the crunch can add to their pain rather than alleviate it.

We can overdo the "put on a happy face" mentality with children also, and make them think they are only acceptable when they are smiling. When they become adults, they will continue this behavior and never come to grips with their negative feelings. We need to remember that "even in laughter the heart may ache" (Prov. 14:13), and not be so determinedly cheerful that we are being hypocritical and asking others to be so also. No one is continuously ecstatic. If someone says, "How are you," and we are feeling terrible, it should be all right, at least some of the time, to say so.

Cheerfulness and Depression

But by far the biggest personality problem is not being too cheerful but being too heavy-hearted. Depression is a common problem, even among Christians. When a person is feeling "down," living is difficult enough. But when someone is severely depressed, life seems hopeless, and he or she feels worthless, unable to face another person or task.

Those who have continuing problems with depression should have a thorough physical examination by a psychiatrist or internist to see if there is a medical cause for their condition. A lithium imbalance, for example, has been found in some people who have marked highs that last for weeks or months followed by severe lows. Women should have regular check-ups with a gynecologist, during which they can explain any unusual moodiness and get help for special problems. If these steps have been taken and depression still exists, the depressed individual should seek a Christian psychologist and get to the root of the problem. Severe depression "dries up the bones," affects family and friends, and hinders our usefulness to the Lord.

Depression can be the result of spiritual problems such as guilt that remains unresolved. We can also be depressed because of the loss of something or someone important to us. Psychologists say that a main cause of depression is repressed hostility. We are angry but do not feel able to express our anger, so we bottle it up inside where it becomes depression. Anger is hard to express in a Christian manner, but we can learn to do so (Eph. 4:26). For the sake of our mental and physical health, we must bring our anger out into the open and learn how to manage it. Since even Christians are sometimes afraid to face their true feelings, the skill of a Christian psychologist can be of great help to us.

We will never be able to consider our hearts cheerful ones while anger, bitterness, and other harmful emotions are bubbling in them. Volcanoes may be described as dangerous, dramatic, or spectacular, but hardly as cheerful.

Godly Cheerfulness

Depressed or sad people are living "under the circumstances," immobilized by something that has happened to them. But God wants us to rise above the circumstances, to rejoice even in hard times. If we want to change and to learn to be content, we can try some of these suggestions:

1. We can start believing Romans 8:28—"And we know that in all things God works for the good of those who love him, who have been called according to his purpose." We need to tell ourselves over and over again that no stranger, employer, family member, or acquaintance can do anything to us that God cannot use for good in our lives. If Joseph could say to the brothers that sold him into slavery, "You

intended to harm me, but God intended it for good . . . "
(Gen. 50:20), we too can learn to trust God's goodness and
power.

2. We can forgive those who have hurt us. Bitterness and
joy cannot dwell together in the heart—one or the other
must leave. If Joseph could find the grace to say to his
brothers, " . . . do not be distressed and do not be angry with
yourselves for selling me here, because it was to save lives
that God sent me ahead of you" (Gen. 45:5), we also can
find the grace from God to forgive those who have misused
us. We can know the release and joy that God intends for us
only if we forgive those who have hurt us.

3. We can face the fact that we alone choose how we
respond. We can choose whether or not an event will ruin
our day. We can ask the Lord to help us react positively, or
we can respond out of our fallen human nature. We can let
sin spread and compound by adding our own sinful reaction
to someone else's sinful action. The responsibility for the
choice is ours.

4. We can confront the situation that is disturbing us. We
can pray for God to give us His control, courage, and love for
the other person. Then we can discuss the situation with the
offender. This may not solve the problem to our complete
satisfaction, but taking positive action will keep us from
feeling like a powerless victim.

5. We can increase our sense of the ridiculous. Most of us
take ourselves far too seriously. If we decide to do so, we can
laugh at the silly aspects of many things that would upset us
otherwise.

A month ago the heavy door of my husband's car swung
shut on my head. My glasses and earrings were knocked off,
and both ears were bloodied, remaining swollen for two
weeks. It wasn't a serious injury, but it was painful, especially
when I tried to wear earrings on my cauliflower ears. Yet I

couldn't keep from chuckling about it every time I thought what a comical picture I must have presented.

When someone comes to us with a ridiculous complaint, we don't need to get in a huff, we can enjoy the humorous side of it and keep the blood pressure down. Our family has a whole collection of sayings that set us all laughing—and they have come from incidents that could have been irritating.

6. We can look for things to laugh at. Read comic strips. Cut out cartoons and pin them on the bulletin board. Encourage people to tell you jokes and share funny incidents with you.

Last week a man in our church sent my husband, a pastor, a large manila envelope marked "Personal and Confidential." Inside was a note: "I know at times you like to get away and be completely anonymous and inconspicuous. I hope these will help." With the note was a pair of phony glasses with bushy black feather eyebrows and mustache, and huge nose attached. He has enjoyed using them several times—when he wanted to be sure not to attract any attention, of course. "A cheerful look brings joy to the heart" (Prov. 15:30).

7. We can look for things to be thankful for. We should not have to lose our health, a loved one, or our home to realize how much they mean to us. Thankfulness should become our basic life attitude, appreciating what we have instead of concentrating on what we do not have. We can expend our energies counting our blessings instead of our complaints.

8. We can refuse to mull problems over and over. Our deep needs should be brought before the Lord in prayer and left with Him. Worry is not action. If there is nothing we can actually do to solve a problem, worrying will not help either. We can use Paul's rule to measure our thoughts: "Finally, brothers, whatever is true, whatever is noble, whatever is

right, whatever is pure, whatever is lovely, whatever is admirable—if anything is excellent or praiseworthy—think about such things" (Phil. 4:8).

9. We can confess our sins. We can realize that worry, ingratitude to God, lack of trust in Him, bitterness, joylessness, all betray a heart that needs to be right before the Lord. We have fallen short of God's purpose for us, and that is sin (Rom. 3:23). We can confess our sins and let God renew our hearts and restore to us the joy of His salvation (Ps. 51:7–12).

A godly heart is a cheerful heart. Satan would like to keep us bound up in sinful, harmful attitudes, but God would free us from such misery and make us His joyful people. "But may the righteous be glad and rejoice before God; may they be happy and joyful" (Ps. 68:3).

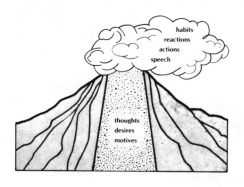

DIGGING DEEPER

1. How would you relate the cheerful heart to the contented heart in chapter 4? _____

_____

What new elements do you find in the cheerful heart? _____

_____

2. a. How do people without God try to put cheer into their lives (Ecclesiastes 2:3–11)? _____

_____

_____

b. What is the result? _____

_____

c. How do Christians get caught up in this same mentality? _____

_____

3. a. Of the people you know, how many have cheerful faces? _____

b. Is Proverbs 15:13a invariably correct? _____

c. Would others classify your face as cheerful? _____

d. What, if anything, should you do about this? _____

_____

4. What does the Christian have to be glad about?

a. Psalm 5:11 _____

b. Psalm 16:8, 9 _____

c. Psalm 21:6 _____

d. Psalm 31:7 _____

e. Psalm 67:4 _____

f. Psalm 92:4–5 _____

g. Psalm 118:24 _____

h. Psalm 122:1 _____

i. Proverbs 23:15, 16 _____

j. Isaiah 25:9 _____

k. Isaiah 65:17, 18 _____

l. Acts 2:46, 47 _____

m. Acts 15:3 _____

n. 1 Corinthians 16:17, 18 _____

What other things can you add to this list? _____

_____

_____

5. What can we learn from how the following people reacted to the circumstances of their lives?

a. Genesis 3:1–6 _____

_____

b. Genesis 13:1–12 _____

_____

c. Ruth 1:1–6, 19–21 (compared with 1:11–18; 2:2)

_____

d. 1 Samuel 24:1–7 _____

_____

e. Job 1:13–22; 7:5, 7; 13:15 _____

_____

f. Jonah 4:6–8 _____

_____

g. Mark 12:41–44 _____

_____

h. Luke 23:33–34 _____

_____

i. Acts 5:40–42 _____

_____

j. Acts 16:19–34 _____

_____

6. In what areas of your life are you living "under the circumstances"? _____

_____

What Scriptures have helped you understand how you can rise above your present situation? _____

_____

_____

7. How can we add joy to our lives?

a. Nehemiah 8:8, 12 _____

b. Psalm 16:11 _____

c. Psalm 19:8; 119:111 _____

d. Psalm 43:5 _____

e. Psalm 81:1, 2; 98:4–9 _____

f. Psalm 100:2 _____

g. Proverbs 12:20 _____

h. Proverbs 15:23 _____

i. John 15:10–11 _____

j. Acts 13:52; Galatians 5:22 _____

k. Philippians 2:2 _____

8. What difference, if any, do you discern between being cheerful, joyful, glad, or happy? _____

_____

_____

_____

9. What can a depressed person learn from Psalm 102? What other Psalms might help? _____

_____

_____

_____

10. What two character traits or attitudes are characteristic of the cheerful heart?

a. Psalm 69:30; 100:4; Ephesians 5:19–20; Colossians 3:16–17; Hebrews 12:28 _____

b. Psalm 31:24; 42:5; 71:14; Acts 2:26; Romans 15:13

_____

11. Do you think your heart could be considered cheerful?

_____

If not, what would the Lord have you do about it? _____

_____

_____

_____

9

A WISE HEART

The wise in heart are called discerning, and pleasant words promote instruction (Prov. 16:21).

One characteristic of life in the 1980s is the incessant demand for more speed. Those who once thought instant coffee and satellite communications were the last word in quickness find instead that they were just the beginning. Everything from photocopying to delivering packages across the country must now be done in minutes or hours instead of days. Computers provide within seconds the answers to complicated problems that would require countless hours of calculating for the best human brains. We have become accustomed to watching today's war on tonight's news and to being informed up-to-the-minute on every issue. The thought of sitting at a stoplight or having to wait until tomorrow for an answer is enough to send some people's blood pressure soaring.

But there are still some things in this world that cannot be achieved in an instant, and one of those is wisdom. Perhaps that is why it is in such short supply. We may know people who are smart, perhaps even a few who could be classified as brilliant. But few of us know many who could be called wise.

When the Bible speaks of wisdom, it is not referring to an accumulation of knowledge, or the possession of common sense, or even the understanding that comes from years of observing human folly. Biblical wisdom is *the ability to apply the Word of God to life situations*. The wise person knows God's principles for living and has the discernment to use them appropriately.

The results of applying mere human wisdom would be laughable if they were not so tragic. A twice-divorced woman psychologist holds classes to help wives learn how to have extra-marital affairs "without harming themselves or others." A fourteen-year-old girl is required to get parental permission to ride a school bus but not to get birth control devices. Tens of thousands of women lobby to pass an Equal Rights Amendment that would nullify the protections in industry that other thousands of women worked for years to achieve. A sports star loses his family and job because of his addiction to cocaine. Without God's truth as a guide, we see again and again that "there is a way that seems right to a man, but in the end it leads to death" (Prov. 16:25).

The Wise Know the Scriptures

There are no instantly wise people because it takes time to know the Bible well enough to apply it properly. This is part of the reason why we are told not to make new believers church officers (1 Tim. 3:6). Also, we cannot know whether people are faithful servants of the Lord until some time has passed. Those who are young in their Christian faith have not had sufficient time to acquire knowledge of the Bible or the wisdom needed for spiritual leadership.

Jesus told people in His day that they had come to erroneous conclusions because they did not know the Scriptures or the power of God (Mark 12:24). This is still true today. Therefore we must be careful that when we get advice or give counsel to others we are not just relying on human insight, but on principles from God's Word. And we cannot know God's Word without studying it. There is no quick fix, no easy injection of biblical knowledge into our minds. We must make the effort to learn it.

This is why there are so few wise people. Those who get all their knowledge of God's Word from an hour or two on Sunday will never have a personal grasp of its content. Paul said that if we want to be wise, if we want to "correctly handle the word of truth," we must be workmen (2 Tim. 2:15). We must do the job ourselves instead of expecting a pastor or teacher to do it all for us. We must read the Bible. We must digest it, meditate on it, memorize it, understand it.

The Wise Are Mature

The writer of the Epistle to the Hebrews was frustrated. He had many wonderful truths he wanted to impart, but his audience did not want to expend much energy on spiritual growth. They had been Christians for some time, but they knew little more than when they first believed. He complains:

> We have much to say about this, but it is hard to explain because you are slow to learn. In fact, though by this time you ought to be teachers, you need someone to teach you the elementary truths of God's word all over again. You need milk, not solid food! Anyone who lives on milk, being still an infant, is not acquainted with the teaching about righteousness. But solid food is for the mature, who by constant use have trained themselves to distinguish good from evil. Therefore let us leave the

elementary teachings about Christ and go on to maturity.
Hebrews 5:11−6:1

Those who feed on and digest the meat of God's Word attain maturity in their Christian lives. They gain the wisdom in speech and action that is the mark of the mature. If we are not mature, the reason is obvious: we have not been "workmen" but idlers in Bible study. We have not made constant use of the Scriptures to distinguish good from evil. We are still dependent on others for our knowledge, as children are, in danger of being misguided by those who sound knowledgeable but may be as ignorant as we.

God does not want us to remain spiritually immature. He wants us to ". . . become mature, attaining to the whole measure of the fullness of Christ. Then we will no longer be infants, tossed back and forth by the waves, and blown here and there by every wind of teaching and by the cunning and craftiness of men in their deceitful scheming. Instead, speaking the truth in love, we will in all things grow up " (Eph. 4:13−15).

The Wise Are Discerning

The ability to detect error, to discriminate between sound and unsound doctrine, to be spiritually astute and perceptive, is called "discernment" in the Bible. Without discernment, women are susceptible to false teachers, to those who have "a form of godliness" but who oppose God, "who worm their way into homes and gain control over weak-willed women " (2 Tim. 3:5, 6).

In contrast, those who feed on the meat of God's Word learn to discern between truth and falsehood. Their ears prick when questionable statements are made. They notice what is left out of a teacher's presentation as well as what is actually taught, for they know that omitting part of the gospel is one way of teaching falsely. They have an alarm system that goes off when a Scripture verse is used incorrectly to prove a point. They do not let the emotion of the moment blind them to the content of the message. They know that any deviation from scriptural truth is a serious matter.

The opposite of truth is not fantasy but falsehood. The opposite of good is not mediocrity but evil. Those who reject God's authority and propose solutions based on human wisdom are not just a little off base but dangerous. "Such 'wisdom' does not come down from heaven but is earthly, unspiritual, of the devil" (James 3:15). Satan, however, has always been able to give his ideas a sugar coating, so that many of his proposals are gullibly swallowed. And since he and his followers can even masquerade themselves as angels of light (2 Cor. 11:13–15), it takes a wise and alert woman to pierce the disguise and discern error and falsehood.

The Wise Are Prudent

Evidence of Satan's success in twisting people's minds is all around us. In the woman psychologist's view (whom we mentioned earlier), prudence means using excuses no one can verify when you are cheating on your husband. To some "pro-choice" people, abortion is a prudent means of birth control. For some office-seekers, any deceit or trickery is prudent if it gets them elected.

Godly prudence, however, is disciplining ourselves to put God's principles to work in our conduct, our speech, and in family and business affairs. The prudent person looks down the road to see what will result from her actions so that she can avoid problems (Prov. 27:12). She is careful with money and takes care of the possessions God has given her; she is a smart shopper and cooks healthy meals for her family (Prov. 31:14–15). She thinks before she speaks and avoids needless controversy (Prov. 12:16, 23). She puts her knowledge of the Bible to use when making her everyday decisions, realizing that they are the proof of the sincerity of her faith and her obedience to God.

The Wise Are Discreet

While prudence tends to relate more to practical and business matters, discretion pertains more to the handling of potentially troublesome interpersonal or social situations. Just as a diplomat is expected to represent his government's position without precipitating a war, so the discreet person is to speak and act in a manner that aids in finding solutions to problems instead of exacerbating them.

Perhaps the greatest failing among women regarding discretion is their inability to keep private information to themselves. The inner pressure they feel from knowing a secret is often so great that they cannot contain themselves, even if divulging it embarrasses or harms another. Women should remember that "like a gold ring in a pig's snout is a beautiful woman who shows no discretion" (Prov. 11:22). A wise woman knows how to handle situations discreetly and can keep her mouth closed about them afterwards.

The Wise Are Self-Controlled

One of the distinguishing qualities of the wise from the foolish is the ability to benefit from instruction and learn self-discipline (Prov. 15:5). The wise can control their emotions, their speech, their actions. Since the heart is the mind (speech), emotions, and will (actions), we can see that wisdom is indeed a matter of the heart.

A woman who wants to be wise must first control her schedule and her desires so that she spends the time in Bible study that is required for growth and maturity. This in itself will make her different from the wordly-wise that reject God's discipline in their lives. Her growth in godly knowledge will increase her discernment and in turn make her aware of specific areas in her life that need more self-control. She will also become more aware of the terrible effects of mere human wisdom as she sees the disintegrating lives around her.

The sad results of living according to human wisdom are so obvious that it is hard to understand how people can continue on in their same blind, stubborn manner. But the Word, to the wise, is sufficient:

> Be very careful, then, how you live—not as unwise but as wise, making the most of every opportunity, because the days are evil.   Ephesians 5:15−16

DIGGING DEEPER

1. What character traits were included in this chapter?

_____

What negative character traits are the opposite of these?

_____

2. Which aspect of the heart—mind, emotion, or will—do you think is mainly involved in the following:

a. The faithful heart _____

b. The diligent heart _____

c. The compassionate heart _____

d. The wise heart _____

3. Read Psalm 19:7−11 to answer the following:

a. What synonyms for "Scripture" do you find? _____

_____

_____

b. What assertions are made regarding the reliability of God's Word? _____

_____

c. What does God's Word do for people? _____

_____

_____

d. How does your attitude toward God's Word compare with that in verse 10? _____

_____

4. For what purposes was the Book of Proverbs written (Proverbs 1:1−6)? _____

_____

_____

5. a. According to Jesus in Matthew 7:24−27, what does the wise person do? _____

_____

b. What does the foolish person do? _____

_____

c. What results from acting wisely? _____

_____

d. From acting foolishly? _____

_____

6. a. How does Satan's deception of Eve in Genesis 3:4−6 relate to the discussion in this chapter? _____

_____

_____

b. How is Satan deceiving people similarly today? _____

_____

_____

c. Where are we supposed to go for wisdom? See Proverbs 1:7; James 1:5. _____

_____

d. What can you learn about God's wisdom vs. the world's wisdom in 1 Corinthians 1:20–31? _____

_____

_____

_____

_____

7. Read Proverbs 19:14. In what ways should a wife be prudent? See Proverbs 31:10–31 for ideas. _____

_____

_____

_____

8. How can the examples of prudence in Luke 14:28–32 be applied to your life? _____

_____

_____

9. How is Christian discretion expressed by Paul in 1 Corinthians 8:4–13? _____

_____

_____

Can you apply this to present day issues? _____

_____

_____

10. In what specific areas are we to display self-control?

   a. Proverbs 10:19; 17:27 _____

_____

   b. Proverbs 16:32; 19:11 _____

_____

   c. Ephesians 5:15–18 _____

_____

   d. 1 Thessalonians 4:3–4 _____

_____

   e. 1 Timothy 2:9 _____

_____

   f. Titus 2:11–13 _____

_____

11. Which do you think characterizes our nation, Deuteronomy 4:5–6, or Deuteronomy 32:28–29? Why do you think so? _____

_____

_____

12. If a person desires with all her heart to become wise, how much time do you think she needs to spend in Bible study? _____

What adjustments, if any, do you need to make in the amount of time you study God's Word? _____

10

A COURAGEOUS HEART

Be strong, and let your heart take courage, all you who hope in the LORD (Ps. 31:24, NASB).

A Christian student faces a derisive teacher and class-mates, trying to think how to defend her beliefs. A couple grapples with the shock of having the husband's employment abruptly terminated. A woman lies on her hospital bed knowing that in a few hours she will have a mastectomy. These are only a sample of the kinds of trials that come to people like you and me everyday, even in a relatively protected environment. Around the world, Christians face graver tests, suffering persecution, imprisonment, and even death. What resources are available for dealing with such crises? How can we face life in the crunch with courageous hearts?

From its opening chapters onward, the Bible repeatedly deals with these questions. The people of the Scriptures experienced every possible type of threat to life, limb, and psyche; their responses and the results of those responses can benefit us today. For their failures "were written down as warnings for us" (1 Cor. 10:11), so that we might avoid their mistakes. Their victories were recorded so we can imitate their faith (Heb. 6:12).

The Origin of Fear

Conditioned as we are to life in a fallen world, it is impossible to conceive of Adam's and Eve's paradise. Everything our hearts yearn for was theirs in full; nothing that alarms us was allowed to disturb their peace. The created world was their friend, not the quaking, flaming, flooding, drought-parched, or storming enemy millions fight today. Adam's and Eve's relationship with each other included no hurt feelings, fear of loss, or physical or emotional harm. Their work was satisfying, accomplished without toil or frustration. Their fellowship with their Creator was character-ized by perfect trust and love. They felt no fear of judgment or discovery, for they were innocent of all wrong-doing. Human enemies did not exist.

But the enemy of the soul did exist, and the moment our first parents gave in to Satan and disobeyed God, fear entered the world. In place of the confident fellowship with God that Adam had known, he told the Lord, "I heard you in the garden, and I was afraid because I was naked; so I hid" (Gen. 3:10). Since that moment humans have known no real peace but have been "harassed at every turn—conflicts on the outside, fears within" (2 Cor. 7:5).

Overcoming Fear

According to the Bible, there is only one way to overcome all the fears that beset us, and that is to trust the Lord. "When I am afraid, I will trust in you. In God, whose word I praise, in God I trust; I will not be afraid. What can mortal man do to me?" (Ps. 56:3, 4).

This simple answer is difficult to put into continuous practice, however. For we know that trusting the Lord does not mean we will necessarily be spared suffering or loss. Believers over the centuries have endured every form of pain and hardship known to man. Jesus made it plain that His followers would experience the same kind of hate and persecution that He did (John 15:18–20).

If trusting God does not mean that we will be spared pain, what does it accomplish? What, exactly, are we supposed to trust Him to do?

1. We can trust that God will be with us in every trial. God obviously felt that this assurance would be enough to calm any fear, for He told Moses, "Be strong and courageous. Do not be afraid or terrified because of them, for the LORD your God goes with you; he will never leave you nor forsake you" (Deut. 31:6; cf. Heb. 13:5). We can know, then, that He could remove the problem if He chose to do so, since He is right there with us.

2. We can trust that God is powerful enough to change anything. He is stronger than all the forces of evil (John 16:33). And if the winds and the waters obey Him (Exod. 14:21; Luke 8:24), if His plans for nations are carried out whether they acknowledge Him or not (Isa. 14:24, 26–27), if He can strike people dead (Acts 12:23) and set men chained in dungeons free (Acts 12:6, 7), then He can rescue us if it is His will.

3. We can trust that God will work everything for our good (Rom. 8:28). If God can use treachery and slavery for good in Joseph's life (Gen. 50:20) and bring good from Job's sufferings (Job 42:10–17), we can believe His promise to us.

4. We can trust that what happens to us is God's will, not man's. If "the LORD foils the plans of the nations; he thwarts the purposes of the peoples. But the plans of the LORD stand firm forever" (Ps. 33:10, 11); if "in his heart a man plans his

course, but the LORD determines his steps" (Prov. 16:9), then we can be assured that no person or group of persons can alter God's will for our lives.

5. We can know that God loves us and that nothing can separate us from that love (Rom. 8:35–39). Jesus said that He loves us (John 15:9) and that the Father loves us (John 16:27). He proved His love for us in the most convincing way, by dying for us. Therefore we can trust God in every circumstance because whatever comes must come in the presence of our loving, all-powerful, faithful, heavenly Father who never forsakes us.

The Meaning of Courage

To be courageous, then, does not mean we do not understand the seriousness of a situation or the danger we are in. Rather it means that, understanding our position, we nevertheless seek to know God's will for us and depend on His leading instead of reacting on the basis of human fear or pressure. Those who do not feel fear in life-threatening situations are not necessarily the courageous ones. The courageous are those who calm their initial fright by acknowledging God's presence, and then act while trusting in the Lord rather than panicking.

The root of the word "courage" is the Latin *cor*, meaning heart. This is interesting, particularly since our study centers on the heart.

When the song says, "You gotta have heart," or someone says, "Take heart," or "I nearly had heart failure," we know what they mean, don't we? We know that it is not love or compassion they are referring to, but the marshaling of our inner resources to meet a challenge or danger. This challenge or danger can be psychological or physical, serious or rather unimportant (such as introducing ourselves to a group of strangers). But whenever our heart starts pounding and that debilitating weakness comes over us, we need to "Wait for the Lord; be strong, and let your heart take courage; yes, wait for the Lord" (Ps. 27:14, NASB).

The Courageous Are Bold

Courage has two aspects. One is defensive—waiting on the Lord, being strong, standing firm against the enemy (1 Cor. 16:13). The other is offensive—being not only stouthearted but bold (Ps. 138:3).

It is this second aspect that is hardest for many of us. We prefer to remain invisible and safe, to avoid taking a stand in a controversy. Instead of being ready to speak up for the Lord (1 Peter 3:15), people have to pry our testimony out of us. We find it hard even to invite them to a church activity. We are so fearful of rebuff or awkwardness that we become fainthearted and shrink from doing or saying what we know we should.

There is only one way to become bold. If we try to force ourselves, we will fail more often than we succeed. But if we pray and trust the Lord, He will make us bold. David said, "When I called, you answered me; you made me bold and stouthearted" (Ps. 138:3). The apostles also prayed for boldness (Acts 4:29).

The point is that prayer takes our minds off our feelings and fears, and focuses them on the Lord and the needs of others. When we concentrate on doing God's will in a challenging situation, our hearts are calmed, and we recognize the power at our disposal. Then we are able to be bold because doing what the Lord wants us to do has become more important than our own nervousness.

The Courageous Are Confident

As we continue to trust God in times of stress, we become confident. We can say, based on our past experience of the strength of God: "being confident of this, that he who began a good work in you will carry it on to completion until the day of Christ Jesus" (Phil. 1:6). We know God will enable us to do anything He calls us to do, and this gives us an assurance that can be seen by others.

We are also confident of our relationship with God. We know that our faith in Jesus Christ saves us and makes us right with the Father. We know God loves us personally and tenderly. Our knowledge that we have instant access to Him, that we can "approach the throne of grace with confidence, so that we may receive mercy and find grace to help us in our time of need" (Heb. 4:16), turns our natural hesitancy into confident action.

The Courageous Encourage Others

As we share our victories and tell others how God has helped us, they are encouraged and made braver. We don't usually think of the word "encourage" as meaning "to impart courage to," but that is what it means. The timid are built up as they hear how God answers prayers for boldness, and they are encouraged to trust God for boldness as well.

This encouragement is one reason why we need to be part of a local body of believers. The Lord did not design us to be "Lone Rangers." We cannot build up one another if we never see each other. That is why we are warned: "Let us not give up meeting together, as some are in the habit of doing, but let us encourage one another—and all the more as you see the Day approaching" (Heb. 10:25). We need to be fortified by the preaching of the Word of God and be strengthened by the faith of others, and they need to hear how the Lord has fought battles for us.

The Courageous Are Hopeful

Paul said it was his hope in the glorious gospel that made him bold (2 Cor. 3:12). Our key verse calls on "all you who hope in the LORD" to "be strong, and let your heart take courage" (Ps. 31:24, NASB). It is our knowledge of God's miraculous power that makes us hopeful even in the darkest moments, because we know He still works miracles of healing and deliverance. We remember all His signs and wonders in the Bible; we recall answers to prayer that have defied human explanations or modern medical science, and we hope in God in the present situation.

This hope is more than earthly wishful thinking that says, "I hope everything turns out all right." It is our confident trust in a God who can do anything that makes us say with David:

> The LORD is my light and my salvation—whom shall I fear? The LORD is the stronghold of my life—of whom shall I be afraid? . . . Though an army besiege me, my heart will not fear; though war break out against me, even then will I be confident. I am still confident of this: I will see the goodness of the LORD in the land of the living. Wait for the LORD; be strong and take heart and wait for the LORD. Psalm 27:1, 3, 13–14

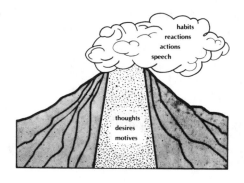

DIGGING DEEPER

1. a. What character traits were included in this chapter?

_____

b. What negative traits are the opposite of each of these?

_____

_____

c. Which areas are involved in these traits: motives, desires, thoughts, speech, actions, reactions, habits? _____

_____

2. How is God described in the following?

a. Genesis 15:1 _____

b. Psalm 27:1 _____

c. Psalm 46:1, 7 _____

d. Hebrews 13:6 _____

How do these designations affect you? _____

_____

3. What are we specifically told we need not fear? What reason for fearlessness does each reference give?

a. Psalm 23:4 _____

_____

b. Psalm 27:1, 3 _____

_____

c. Psalm 46:1–3 _____

_____

d. Psalm 112:1, 7 _____

_____

e. Proverbs 3:25, 26 _____

_____

f. Isaiah 51:7,12 _____

_____

g. Jeremiah 10:5 _____

_____

h. Luke 12:4 _____

_____

i. Revelation 2:10 _____

_____

Which of these are the greatest sources of fear for you?

_____

4. What would you reply to someone who says God promises His children peaceful, prosperous, trouble-free lives? _____

_____

_____

5. a. What could be the purposes of trials? See James 1:2–4; 1 Peter 1:6, 7. _____

_____

_____

b. What is to be our attitude in tribulation (Matthew 5:10–12)? _____

_____

c. Is this a matter of mind, will, emotion, or all three? Why? _____

_____

_____

d. Do you think this attitude is possible for you? Why?

_____

6. a. What do you learn about responding to persecution from Acts 16:19–34? _____

_____

b. What tells you that God could have prevented their beating if He had willed? _____

_____

c. According to this passage, what can result from persecution? _____

_____

7. a. What image is used to describe the Christian life in 2 Corinthians 10:3–4 and 2 Timothy 2:3–4? _____

_____

b. How does this compare with your attitude toward life? _____

_____

c. What hymns deal with this image? _____

_____

_____

8. What are the guidelines for a Christian's strategy in 2 Corinthians 10:3–5? _____

_____

_____

What do you think are the "weapons of the world" that we should not use? (Include 1 Peter 2:21–23 in your answer.)

_____

_____

What are our targets? _____

_____

_____

9. What do you learn in Ephesians 6:10–18 about the following:

a. What kind of strength to seek

b. Who the enemy is, is not

c. Why put on God's protection

d. What God's protection consists of

e. Why each piece is necessary

f. How this helps promote courage

10. What aids boldness?

    a. Acts 4:13 _____

    b. Acts 9:31 _____

    c. Romans 1:12; 1 Thessalonians 3:7,8 _____

    d. Romans 15:4 _____

    e. Romans 15:5 _____

    f. Ephesians 6:19–20 _____

    g. 1 Thessalonians 3:2 _____

11. a. If 2 Timothy 1:7 is true, where does fear come from?

_____

    b. What idea does Mark 4:40 add? _____

_____

    c. When we are overcome with fear, how can John 14:27 help us? _____

_____

12. Make a list of things Christians can do to encourage each other (use 1 Thessalonians 5:11, 14 in your answer).

_____

_____

Use one of these to encourage a fellow believer, and share the results with your group.

13. How does the following hymn by Martin Luther help you to have a more courageous heart?

A Mighty Fortress Is Our God

A mighty Fortress is our God, A Bulwark never failing;
Our Helper he amid the flood Of mortal ills prevailing.
For still our ancient foe Doth seek to work us woe;
His craft and pow'r are great; And, armed with cruel hate,
On earth is not his equal.

Did we in our own strength confide, Our striving would be losing;

Were not the right Man on our side, The Man of God's own choosing.

Dost ask who that may be? Christ Jesus, it is he;

Lord Sabaoth his Name, From age to age the same,

And he must win the battle.

And though this world with devils filled, Should threaten to undo us,

We will not fear, for God hath willed His truth to triumph through us.

The prince of darkness grim, We tremble not for him;

His rage we can endure, For lo! his doom is sure;

One little word shall fell him.

That Word above all earthly powers, No thanks to them abideth;

The Spirit and the gifts are ours Through him who with us sideth;

Let goods and kindred go, This mortal life also;

The body they may kill: God's truth abideth still;

His kingdom is for ever.

11

A PURE HEART

Blessed are the pure in heart, for they will see God (Matt. 5:8).

If someone were to ask you what God requires of His children, what would you answer? The question itself is shocking, for few seem to care any more what God thinks about anything. If the average person has given any thought to the matter at all, he or she has probably concluded that God is tolerant of human foibles and lax in enforcing His standards. The prevailing attitude mirrors that of the scoffers predicted by Peter: "Where is this 'coming' he promised? Ever since our fathers died, everything goes on as it has since the beginning of creation" (2 Peter 3:4).

But God's basic requirement is still in force. The standard He set for the Hebrews (Deut. 6:5) is the same command reiterated by Jesus for people living thousands of years later: "Love the Lord your God with all your heart and with all your soul and with all your mind and with all your strength" (Mark 12:30).

Perhaps it is the total impossibility of meeting such a requirement that causes people to back off and decide that God cannot be serious. Even to Christians the idea of having a pure heart—of loving God with all the heart, soul, mind, and strength—sounds like a task for a fanatic, or for someone shut away from the world we deal with everyday. Our mental computers flash "error" as we try to link the word "pure" with human beings.

God's Solution

Of course God is infinitely more aware of our limitations than we are. He created us, and "he knows how we are formed, he remembers that we are dust" (Ps. 103:14). And since He realizes that fallen human beings can never meet His standard on their own, He provides a remedy for their sins ("foibles"). For the Hebrew, He required the sacrifice of an animal. The procedure of slaughtering a lamb or bull, turning a healthy living thing into a bloody dead one, was supposed to impress upon God's people that sin causes death.

But people can get used to anything, and after a while, animal sacrifices lost their impact for many. Some people began bringing diseased animals to the altar; others became indifferent to their sin and ceased sacrificing altogether. Then, in the fullness of time, Jesus, the true Lamb of God, came to make the perfect sacrifice for your sins and mine. For those of us who believe and receive the Lord Jesus Christ, His blood cleanses us from all sin and makes us pure before God.

> Day after day every priest stands and performs his religious duties; again and again he offers the same sacrifices, which can never take away sins. But when this priest had offered for all time one sacrifice for sins, he sat

down at the right hand of God. . . . because by one
sacrifice he has made perfect forever those who are
being made holy.   Hebrews 10:11,12,14

Positional vs. Practical Sanctification

In the opening pages of this study, we defined "sanctification" as spiritual growth, our increase in holiness,
becoming more like Christ our Savior. But there is another,
even stronger meaning of the word. The word "sanctify"
literally means to set something or someone aside for a holy
use or purpose, or to make something or someone holy. On
the one hand, we know we are imperfect (failing but growing
Christians), while on the other hand we are considered
already perfect in God's sight. The purity and holiness of
Jesus Christ has been imputed or attributed to us. This
imputed holiness is our *positional* sanctification, the position
in which we stand blameless because of Christ's blame-
lessness. But as a practical matter, we are still sinners with a
long way to go in our growth in sanctification.

The Bible exhorts us to pursue sanctification, to become
increasingly holy in our living (Rom. 12:1; Heb.
12:14) while also proclaiming the wonderful news that we
are both justified and sanctified already in God's sight
(1 Cor. 6:11). What we could never do for ourselves, God
has done for us in Christ Jesus: "He has made perfect forever
those who are being made holy" (Heb. 10:14).

Two Reactions

When we really understand that all our sins—past,
present, and future—are forgiven (Heb. 10:17–18) and that
we are holy in God's sight, we may feel such a rush of love
and gratitude toward the One who made it possible that we
dedicate ourselves even more fully to a godly lifestyle. We
feel relief from the fear of judgment that our continuing

transgressions caused. We find ourselves able to confess our sins more freely to God because we know the penalty for them is already paid. Our fellowship with the Father, no longer hindered by our unconfessed sins, blossoms into something that approaches the love of heart, soul, mind, and strength that God desires of us.

However, there is another possible response to our positional righteousness. We may begin to presume upon the mercy and grace of God and become careless in our Christian walk. We may decide that since our place with God is assured, we can "get by" with worldly actions and live less restricted lives.

But this kind of thinking shows little understanding of spiritual things. Living by the world's standards does not bring happiness but disintegration. Neither can we have the Holy Spirit within us and still thoroughly enjoy ungodly activities.

> Do you not know that your body is a temple of the Holy Spirit, who is in you, whom you have received from God? You are not your own; you were bought at a price. Therefore honor God with your body.
>
> 1 Corinthians 6:19–20

Pure Heart, Undivided Heart

To be pure, our hearts must be undivided (Ps. 86:11). We must be loyal to the Lord, faithful servants to Him alone. If we desire pure hearts, we cannot try to keep one foot in the world and one in the kingdom of God. Jesus said that no one can serve two masters at the same time (Matt. 6:24). When Jesus was tempted by the devil to worship him in exchange for all the kingdoms of the world, Jesus answered, "It is written: 'Worship the Lord your God and serve him only'" (Luke 4:8).

When anything is pure, it is free from all contaminants. It takes a diligent heart to detect and remove the pollutants that so easily destroy purity.

Sexual Purity

The kind of impurity most often mentioned in the Bible is sexual impurity. The reason for this is obvious if we think for a moment about the lives of the people of the Bible. Men who trusted God in everything else, including life and death situations, failed to control their sexual desires and fell into sin. This area of our lives often seems to be the first target of the devil's fiery darts, our most vulnerable point. A look around us, perhaps even a look within, will tell us how very successful Satan has been.

But God's standards of purity do not change just because "everybody else is doing it." Rather, "it is God's will that you should be sanctified: that you should avoid sexual immorality. . . . For God did not call us to be impure, but to live a holy life. Therefore, he who rejects this instruction does not reject man but God, who gives you his Holy Spirit" (1 Thess. 4:3, 7, 8).

If we allow sexual impurity in our thought lives, we already have heart trouble, but it can still be treated before it causes permanent damage. We need to be reminded that thoughts and desires easily become speech and actions, that sin compounds and spreads. Impure thoughts must be cleansed from our lives through repentance and confession before they surface in deeds, because not only our reputation but also that of all believers suffers. "But among you there must not be even a hint of sexual immorality, or of any kind of impurity, or of greed, because these are improper for God's holy people" (Eph. 5:3).

Pure Heart, Clear Conscience

If we would have a pure heart, all sin, whether in the past or present, must be rooted out and dealt with so that we can " . . . keep hold of the deep truths of the faith with a clear conscience" (1 Tim. 3:9). We cannot haul a cargo of guilt around with us and still live a joyful Christian life. If we have wronged people, we must get right with them before we can have the inner peace that accompanies a pure heart.

Jesus knew that we cannot concentrate on anything, we cannot even worship properly, if we have a guilty conscience. He said, "Therefore, if you are offering your gift at the altar and there remember that your brother has something against you, leave your gift there in front of the altar. First go and be reconciled to your brother; then come and offer your gift" (Matt. 5:23–24).

Satan loves to interrupt our times of worship and fellowship with the Lord by bringing to our minds dirty stories, memories of scenes from movies, anything that can distract and shatter the spiritual impact of the moment. If we have things on our conscience that we have not settled, he will surely use these to our detriment also. Instead of continuing to harbor unresolved sins, "let us draw near to God with a sincere heart in full assurance of faith, having our hearts sprinkled to cleanse us from a guilty conscience" (Heb. 10:22).

Pure Heart, Holy Life

If our hearts are pure, the rest of our lives will be pure also. Our habits and reactions, our desires and motives will reflect our sanctification. We will be humble not only in our actions but also in our thoughts. Our contentment will be exhibited in our speech as well as felt in our inner desires. Our compassion will not only be godly in the deeds themselves but also in the motives behind the acts. Our diligence in detail will be mirrored by the care we take of the hidden places of our hearts. The wisdom that we offer others will be lived out in our relationships with the members of our own families.

The world is filled with troubled people—people with so much hurt, turmoil, and sin beneath the thin veneer of their lives that they spread chaos and pain wherever they go. The woman of godly character stands in contrast, a balm to the wounds of the world, and a source of strength and encouragement to all who come her way.

She knows that "the LORD searches every heart and understands every motive behind the thoughts" (1 Chron. 28:9), but she is not afraid. For she trusts, not in her own holiness, but in the Lord, "being confident of this, that he who began a good work in you will carry it on to completion until the day of Christ Jesus" (Phil. 1:6).

> May God himself, the God of peace, sanctify you through and through. May your whole spirit, soul and body be kept blameless at the coming of our Lord Jesus Christ. The one who calls you is faithful and he will do it.
>
> 1 Thessalonians 5:23–24

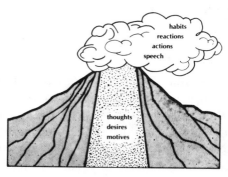

DIGGING DEEPER

1. How does the concept of the pure heart relate to the other "hearts" in this study? _____

_____

_____

2. a. What happens to our physical hearts when impurities enter the blood stream? _____

_____

    b. What other things affect our physical hearts? _____

_____

_____

    c. What dangers to our spiritual hearts could these illustrate? _____

_____

_____

3. What must be kept pure?

    a. Psalm 24:3,4 _____

    b. Psalm 119:9 _____

    c. Proverbs 20:11 _____

    d. Philippians 4:8 _____

    e. 1 Thessalonians 2:3 _____

    f. Titus 1:15 _____

    g. Hebrews 13:4 _____

    h. James 1:27 _____

4. Read Hebrews 12:4–15 and answer the following:

a. How hard are we supposed to fight sin? _____

_____

b. What happens if we allow impurities in our lives? ____

_____

c. How does this treatment show our position with God?

_____

_____

d. What is this treatment designed to help us share? ____

_____

e. What is the fruit of discipline? _____

_____

f. What are the positive ways we can react to God's discipline? _____

_____

g. What are the negative ways? _____

_____

h. Examine your life to see if there are any negative reactions to God's efforts to purify you._____

_____

i. What would you need to do to change your response?

_____

5. What do the following tell you about the hidden areas of our hearts?

a. Psalm 51:6 _____

b. Psalm 94:11 _____

c. Proverbs 16:2 _____

d. Proverbs 17:3 _____

e. 1 Corinthians 4:5 _____

f. Hebrews 4:12–13 _____

6. What does God's Word have to do with our sanctification?

a. Psalm 119:9,11 _____

_____

b. John 15:3 _____

_____

c. John 17:17 _____

_____

d. Hebrews 4:12 _____

_____

e. 1 Peter 2:2 _____

_____

7. a. What types of sin are mentioned in Psalm 19:12,13?

_____

b. Does a clear conscience mean we are sinless? (See Proverbs 16:2; 1 Corinthians 4:4.) _____

_____

c. What should be our prayer? (See Psalm 139:23–24; 51:2.) _____

_____

8. When will every believer be pure, holy, and blameless in fact, as well as in God's sight? (See 1 Thessalonians 3:13; 1 John 3:2.) _____

_____

9. What will result from our efforts to achieve a godly character?

    a. Romans 15:5, 6 _____

_____

    b. 2 Thessalonians 1:11–12 _____

_____

    c. 2 Peter 1:5–11 _____

_____

_____

_____